Affirmative Action

List of Contributors

Richard Young, University of Texas at San Antonio
Jeffrey Prager, University of California-Los Angeles, and the
Institute for Advanced Studies
W.R. Newell, University of Nebraska-Lincoln
Tom W. Rice, University of Vermont
Kenneth Whitby, University of South Carolina
William P. Bridges, University of Illinois at Chicago
Wayne J. Villemez, University of Illinois at Chicago
Lee Sigelman, University of Kentucky
N. Joseph Cayer, Arizona State University
Peter K. Eisinger, University of Wisconsin-Madison
Grace Hall Saltzstein, University of California-Riverside
Jeremy Plant, George Mason University
Frank J. Thompson, University of Georgia
Michael B. Preston, University of Illinois

Affirmative Action

Theory, Analysis, and Prospects

Edited by
Michael W. Combs
and
John Gruhl

McFarland & Company, Inc, Publishers
Jefferson, North Carolina, and London

Acknowledgments

This collection of essays consists of selected papers that were presented at the Eighth Annual Hendricks Symposium which was sponsored by the Department of Political Science, University of Nebraska-Lincoln. The Symposium focused upon the affirmative action controversy. The authors are deeply grateful to Susan Welch and the Department of Political Science at the University of Nebraska for the various resources that were made available. The authors are further indebted to Diane LeNoir, Joyce Miller, Kathleen O'Connor, and Luisa Colón in the Text Processing Center of the College of Arts and Sciences, Louisiana State University for typing the final draft. We are also appreciative of the support provided by our families. —Michael W. Combs and John Gruhl.

Library of Congress Cataloguing-in-Publication Data

Affirmative action.

"Consists of selected papers that were presented at the Eighth Annual Hendricks Symposium which was sponsored by the Department of Political Science, University of Nebraska—Lincoln"—Acknowledgments.
  Includes bibliographies and index.
  1. Affirmative action programs—United States—Congresses. I. Combs, Michael W., 1950– . II. Gruhl, John, 1947– . III. Hendricks Symposium (8th : 1983 : University of Nebraska–Lincoln). IV. University of Nebraska–Lincoln. Dept. of Political Science.
  HF5549.5.A34A47 1986   331.13'3'0973   86-147

ISBN 0-89950-230-X (acid-free natural paper)

Printed in the United States of America

McFarland   Box 611   Jefferson, North Carolina 28640

Table of Contents

Part IV: The Future of Affirmative Action

Introduction

This collection of essays presents theoretical and analytical discussions of anti-discrimination efforts in the area of public and private employment. Specifically, while some attention is devoted to the effects of Title VII of the Civil Rights Act of 1964 which embodies the concept of equal employment opportunity, our major emphasis is upon the principle of affirmative action. Because of the sharp disagreement as to a specific description of affirmative action, here we provide one. By affirmative action, we refer to a set of specific and result-oriented procedures that are utilized to insure that non-whites and women are not disadvantaged in efforts to secure employment (e.g., recruitment, selection, retention, and promotion). The intent of such procedures is to promote and achieve equal employment opportunity, that is, affirmative action is not an end, but rather a means of insuring the ultimate goal of equality of employment opportunity. This is the rationale for requiring employers to monitor the success of affirmative action measures (Flemming, Gill and Swinton, 1978: Chapter 1). The rationale of these procedures is to remedy past and present discrimination against blacks, other minorities and women. Thus, affirmative action is a remedial measure.

Since its inception in the 1960s, however, affirmative action has been a much debated issue. Few issues in the annals of American politics have provoked such sharp, and diverse points of view. The issue has appeared on the agenda of the Congress, the President, and the docket of the Supreme Court, and it has occupied and continues to occupy a salient place in state and local politics. The intensive and pervasive nature of the debate may be attributed to two interrelated factors.

First, in many circles, affirmative action is termed a perversion of the values of the American social and political order. That is, the very concept of affirmative action is thought to fly in the face of some of America's most cherished and deeply held values (e.g., individualism, merit, fairness, and equality). Subsequently, the embracement of the policy of affirmative action creates devastating breaches in the American value system. These breaches produce ill consequences for the victims and the beneficiaries (minorities and women) of affirmative action programs. One of the breaches is reverse discrimination against white males, who, it is argued, are asked to bear the brunt of affirmative action programs, while the eradicated grievances are not of their making. Another negative consequence is the stigmatization of minorities and women; that is creating and reinforcing stereotypes that successful minorities and women have been unfairly aided and that they are less competent than comparable white males. In short, it is argued that individual worth is absent or has been significantly undermined (See generally, Glazer, 1975).

Moreover, it is argued that the time has come for minorities, especially blacks, and women to discontinue their posture of special wards of the government. That is, minorities and women must have their rights protected in the same manner as other citizens (See Livingston, 1979). Specifically, the federal government and special laws have done all that such entities can do to aid such groups. This line of thought grievously reminds one of Justice Bradley's assertion in the Civil Rights Cases of 1883. Justice Bradley insisted that:

> When a man has emerged from slavery, and by the aid of beneficient legislation has shaken off the inseparable concomitants of that state, there must be some stage in the progress of his elevation when he takes the rank of a mere citizen and ceases to be the special favorite of the laws, when his rights as a citizen, or a man are to be protected in the ordinary modes by which other men's rights are protected (Civil Rights Cases 109 U.S. 3, 24 (1883).

The over-riding theme is that enough has been done through legislation, that the discriminatoreal barriers have been removed, and that traditional support from the government to secure equal employment opportunity for minorities and women encroaches upon the constitutional rights of other citizens, especially white males.

Second, while supporters of affirmative action have no quarrels with individualism, merit, fairness, and equality, the source of their concern is that these values have been historically enforced and observed unevenly. Racial and sexual discrimination have infiltrated the American value system, preventing the unbiased application of individualism and other values to blacks and women. This unequal treatment has produced a legacy which continues to shackle minorities and women in their quest for employment, for promotion, and for the retention of jobs. This shackling of blacks and other minorities has forfeited the "color-blind" status of the Constitution. The Constitution has not been interpreted and applied in a racially neutral manner. It was the Supreme Court's interpretation of the Constitution that legitimized Jim Crowism through the "separate but equal" doctrine (Plessy v. Ferguson, 163 U.S. 537, 1896). In fact, the "color-blind" phrase was put forth by Justice Harlan in a dissent from the Court's opinion in Plessy v. Ferguson which established the "separate but equal" doctrine. Plessy and other interpretations of the Constitution by the Supreme Court reflected the social mores and climate of this nation (Bell, 1983). This climate persisted until Brown v. Board of Education (347 U. S. 483 (1954)), when the court overturned the "separate but equal" doctrine. Still, substantive barriers blocked the opportunities of minorities (See Young, this volume). Thus minorities have been and are handicapped or blocked from pursuing their career objectives (See generally, Livingston, 1979).

These blockades have been experienced on both the individual and group levels. For example, it has not been uncommon for the principles that defined all blacks to be applied to each black without regard to ability, level of competence or aspirations (Barnett, 1976: 20). Nevertheless, proof of individual discrimination has become a salient issue in the affirmative action controversy. In Regents of University of California v. Bakke, Justice Marshall addresses this contention, proof of individual discrimination, with unusual candor and historical insight. Marshall argues:

> ...(Blacks) have been discriminated against, not as individuals, but rather solely because of the color of their skins. It is unnecessary in 20th century America to have individual (Blacks) demonstrate that they have been victims of racial discrimination; the racism of our society has been so pervasive that none, regardless of wealth or position, has managed to escape its impact. The experience of (Blacks) in America has been

different in kind, not just in degree, from
that of other ethnic groups (Bakke, 438 U.S.
265, 400, 1978).

As one might expect, Justice Marshall's words were not
the last ones spoken on the point. In fact, the requirement of
proof of individual violations has gained considerable currency
since Bakke. This line of reasoning received implicit support in
Fullilove v. Klutznick, where the Supreme Court sustained a
congressional set-aside program for minority contractors. The
Supreme Court noted that the administrative guidelines of the
set-aside program "provided that a minority business could not
be maintained in the program, even when owned and controlled
by members of the identified minority groups, if it appeared
that the business had not been deprived of the opportunity to
develop and maintain a competitive position in the economy
because of social or economic disadvantage" (Fullilove v.
Klutznick 400 U. S. 400, 464, 1980).

The veiled implications of Fullilove were nearly unmasked
in Firefighters Local Union No. 1784 v. Statts (104 S. Ct. 2576,
1984). In this case, the Supreme Court strongly suggested that
before an affirmative action program can be put in place there
must be proof that the beneficiaries are actual victims. This
litigation grew out of the efforts of a federal district court to
modify a consent decree which required the city of Memphis,
Tennessee to take affirmative steps to increase the proportion
of minority workers in the city's fire department. In 1981, the
federal district court enjoined the Memphis Fire Department
from employing its seniority system so as to disproportionately
lay off minority employees. The Supreme Court reversed the
federal district court (Harvard Law Review 98, 1984: 267).

The Statts decision has provided ammunition to the Reagan
administration assault on affirmative action. The Justice
Department filed several suits in federal courts, challenging the
permissibility of affirmative action programs. William Bradford
Reynolds, head of the Civil Rights Division in the Justice
Department, urged that "(affirmative action is) demeaning
because it says people are getting ahead not because of what
they can do, but because of their race" (Time, 1985: 19). The
action of the Reagan administration signals a significant
reduction in the support of affirmative action. While
affirmative action has received lukewarm support in recent
years, this is the first time that the resources of the Justice
Department have been mobilized and employed to restrict the
application of affirmative programs.

Thus, we are faced with the question whether affirmative
action will continue to be a national policy. This volume
provides significant insights into the need for affirmative

action.   Part I, "American Values and Affirmative Action,"
examines the prevailing American political philosophy of
democratic liberalism and its receptivity to affirmative action.
Richard Young distinguishes procedural and substantive racism.
While affirmative action is a means to overcome substantive
racism, because of the unlikelihood of the proponents of
affirmative action forging a majority, he calls for an expansion
of employment possibilities.   Young argues that economic
prosperity would resolve   the conflict over affirmative action.
Jeffrey Prager addresses the relationship between liberalism's
emphasis upon individual rights and affirmative action's
emphasis upon group rights.   From these two emphases, Prager
attempts to establish a better understanding of the concepts of
merit and qualifications.   Prager concludes that merit is not a
"single" or "one-dimensional" standard, suggesting that present
admission standards are far too restrictive.   Randy Newell
provides an insightful critique of the articles by Young and
Prager.   Then Newell examines the liberal tradition of political
philosophy to consider how the liberal tradition might explicate
the assumptions underlying arguments for and against
affirmative action.   The liberal philosophers analyzed are John
Locke, Jean-Jacques Rousseau and John Rawls.   He concludes
that under certain conditions a place can be found for
affirmative action in liberalism.

        In Part II, "Some Consequences of Equal Employment
Legislation," the focus is upon equal employment opportunity
legislation and how it has affected employment rates, and the
relationship between educational attainment and job
opportunities.   Rice and Whitby examine the differential
between the black and white employment force before and after
the Civil Rights Act of 1964.   The authors found that between
1964 and 1976 there was a period of improvement in black
employment relative to whites; but beginning in 1977, they
observed a continuing pattern of deterioration.   Bridges and
Villimez seek to determine to what extent, if any, minorities are
able to obtain jobs that make full use of their existing
educational achievements.   While the existence of EEOC
coverage has some effect, the effect varies in terms of size of
the employer; moreover, the authors maintain that government
units are consistently less likely than the private sector to
under-employ blacks relative to whites.

        Part III, "The Public Sector and Affirmative Action: An
Assessment," presents a varied analysis of affirmative action
programs in the public sector. Sigelman and Cayer analyze the
employment of minorities and women in all levels of government
from 1973-1980.   The authors argue that minorities and women
continue to lag behind white males in terms of salary received
and positions.   And, while women have fared better in state or

county governments, minorities have done better in federal and municipal governments. Using a sample of large- and medium-size local governments, Peter Eisinger examines a variety of economic transformations (e.g., population growth, per capita revenue growth, growth of manufacturing jobs and federal aid) and black employment. Eisinger finds that the economic transformations that have the most salient effect on black employment are population growth and growth of per capita local revenues. Grace Saltzstein endeavors to determine how and in what ways civil service and affirmative action procedures affect the employment of women in municipal government. Saltzstein finds that cities with veteran preferences, with the rule of three and with antiquated merit systems are associated with lower levels of female employment, while cities with a centralized personnel system, with an affirmative action officer housed in the mayor's office and with an early adopted affirmative action plan have higher levels of female employment.

And, in Part IV, "The Future of Affirmative Action," the authors examine the impact of deregulation on affirmative action and the survival chances of affirmative action given the antagonism of the Reagan administration. Plant and Thompson explore the potential paths of deregulation at the EEOC, discuss why deregulation at the EEOC might focus on enforcement rather than rule revocation, and examine the resources that the White House might use in pursuing an enforcement course of deregulation at the EEOC. The authors indicate that perception of diminished enforcement has emerged under the Reagan administration. Finally, Michael Preston argues that affirmative action will survive the Reaganites -- but it will survive at a cost: the policy is likely to be watered down by the courts and underenforced by the Reagan administration. Preston also contends that the perceptions of hostility to affirmative action may well be more damaging than actual changes in policy.

In sum, while affirmative action is a controversial policy, the findings of this volume reveal that affirmative action is needed to insure the employment opportunities of all Americans.

April 1986   Michael W. Combs

REFERENCES

Barnett, Marguerite R. 1976. "A Theoretical Perspective on American Racial Public Policy." Public Policy for the Black

Community: Strategies and Perspectives. Marguerite R.
Barnett and James A. Hefner, eds. New York: Alfred
Publishing Co.

Bell, Derrick A. 1980. Race, Racism, and American Law.
Boston, MA: Little, Brown and Co.

Flemming, John E., Gerald R. Gill and David H. Swinton. 1978.
The Case for Affirmative Action for Blacks in Higher
Education. Washington, D.C.: Howard University Press.

Glazer, Nathan. 1978. Affirmative Discrimination: Ethnic
Inequality and Public Policy. New York: Basic Books, Inc.

Harvard Law Review 98, 1984: 267.

Livingston, John C. 1979. Fair Game? Inequality and
Affirmative Action. San Francisco, CA: W.H. Freeman and
Company.

Steel, Lewis M. 1971. "Nine Men in Black Who Think White."
Law and Change: In Modern America. Joel B. Grossman
and Mary Grossman, eds. Palisades, CA: Goodyear
Publishing Co.

Thomas, Evan. 1985. "Assault on Affirmative Action." Time,
p. 18.

Part I
American Values and Affirmative Action

Richard Young

Affirmative Action and the
Problem of Substantive Racism*

It is the best of times and the worst of times in black America. The last two decades have witnessed the end of de jure racial segregation and black disfranchisement, the establishment of federal guarantees of equality of opportunity in employment and housing, and the achievement of significant social and economic gains by the black middle class. Nevertheless, the black unemployment rate continues to be double the white rate, and the median black family income is less than three-fifths of the median white family income. Residential segregation and white prejudice persist, as does the physical and social deterioration of the nation's racial ghettos. The socioeconomic gap between the black underclass and the rest of society continues to widen.

These contradictory social trends provide the context for my discussion of the role affirmative action can play in the reduction of racist practices in employment. However, before this task can be undertaken, I first need to define two terms which are central to the analysis which follows: "affirmative action" and "racism."

The term "affirmative action" has been used in many senses, ranging from the prohibition of racial and sexual discrimination in hiring procedures to the initiation of remedial action to compensate for past racist and sexist practices. There are at least four approaches to the problem of discrimination which have been labeled affirmative action:

* The preparation of this paper was made possible by a National Endowment for the Humanities Fellowship for Independent Study and Research and the editorial assistance of Ann Young.

9

1. <u>Passive nondiscrimination.</u> This approach means that the employer refrains from racial or sexual discrimination when choosing among the applicants for a position.

2. <u>Active nondiscrimination.</u> This term implies that the employer will aggressively recruit black, brown, female, and other minority applicants before making an employment decision on the basis of merit.

3. <u>Restitutional nondiscrimination.</u> In this instance, the employer has been guilty of racial, ethnic, or sexual discrimination in the past; in the future, preference will be given to applicants from groups previously discriminated against in order to compensate for past actions.

4. <u>Reverse discrimination.</u> Here, the employer may not have been guilty of past discriminatory practices, but as a matter of policy gives preference in hiring to the members of targeted groups which have experienced discrimination in American society in the past.

Proponents of affirmative action argue that it involves far more than passive nondiscrimination (Benokraitis and Feagin, 1978:1,23), while critics of affirmative action assert that reverse discrimination is a form of racism and sexism directed against white males (Sasseen, 1979:173-190). These different connotations of affirmative action have produced a great deal of public misunderstanding as well as heated legal and philosophical debates. (Gross, 1977; Blackstone and Heslep, 1977)[1]

The word "racism" has also engendered confusion and controversy (Jones, 1972)[2]. For the purposes of this paper, it is useful to distinguish between two types of racism: procedural and substantive (Carmichael and Hamilton, 1967; Knowles and Prewitt, 1969; and Wilson, 1973)[3]. Procedural racism denies the members of subordinate races equality of opportunity; substantive racism denies them equality of condition. Procedural racism is a system in which the members of subordinate racial groups are explicitly denied political, economic, social, and/or cultural opportunities because of their race. Substantive racism is a process by which members of subordinate racial groups are denied these opportunities because of the handicaps of poverty and ignorance. Procedural racism involves the conscious decision by members of the dominant race to discriminate against members of the subordinate race. Substantive racism may involve no discriminatory intent at all. In a society like the United States where the dominant race is a majority of the population, procedural racism can be abolished without disturbing patterns of substantive racism. This century has seen the outlawing of procedural racism in the United States, but substantive racism persists. Both morally and analytically, it is important to remember that contemporary patterns of substantive racism in America are the direct result of the past institutionalization of procedural racism.

The fundamental problem facing black America today is the reality of substantive racism. Racial prejudice and discrimination persist, but they are no longer buttressed by public law or justified by the dominant culture. Today, the black underclass is not imprisoned by Jim Crow practices but by its own social, cultural, political, and economic isolation. This fact does not imply that the black poor are to be blamed for their own plight, but it does mean that the external causes of their suffering are invisible to most white Americans. In a society like the United States in which ethical questions are viewed in terms of intentions rather than consequences, social problems caused by past injustices are particularly intractable.

Forty years ago, Gunnar Myrdal argued in his monumental and extremely influential study of American race relations, An American Dilemma, that "Negroes in their fight for equality have their allies in the white man's own conscience" (Myrdal, 1944: 1009). Myrdal's central thesis was that procedural racism was in conflict with the American Creed of liberal democracy and individual freedom. However, he was unconcerned about the reality of substantive racism. Myrdal argued that

> there is nothing wrong with economic inequality by itself. The mere fact that the Negro people are poorer than other population groups does not per se constitute a social problem. It does not challenge the American Creed. (Myrdal, 1944: 214)

Myrdal's cherished Creed has become a major barrier to a successful assault on the problems of the black underclass, because black poverty does not engender white guilt unless it is the direct result of overt racial discrimination. Thus, in the 1980s, an ideology which is ahistorical, individualistic, and hostile to governmental intervention in social affairs contributes to the perpetuation of substantive racism, no matter how benign white racial beliefs are in the abstract. Today, America's racial dilemma is not a problem of white conscience, but a reality of black poverty and powerlessness, and this reality will not be eliminated by simply prohibiting racist practices.

The problem of substantive racism must be understood in its full complexity if effective strategies are to be devised for its abolition. American race relations need to be seen as more than a function of white racial attitudes; they must be viewed as a consequence of the structure of the American political economy. These precepts mean that measures designed to reduce black poverty must be judged primarily in terms of their political realism and social efficacy.   Thus, in assessing affirmative action programs, we need to look beyond the programs themselves to their ostensible goal: the reduction of black unemployment and underemployment. And we need to ask: Is affirmative action a realistic strategy for eliminating the barriers which prevent many blacks from finding adequate employment? Before this question can be answered, the nature of these barriers must be examined.

The success of a black applicant (or any applicant) in seeking employment is determined by three key variables:(1) applicant competency (Is the applicant qualified for the job?); (2) employer bias (Is the employer actively or passively biased in his employment procedures?); and (3) employment availability (Is an appropriate job available?). The debate over affirmative action usually centers on the first two factors with advocates emphasizing the problem of employer bias and opponents focusing on the issue of applicant competency.

At times, the controversy over affirmative action has become narrowly polemical involving personal attacks and the questioning of motives. For example, some advocates of affirmative action have viewed analyses of black employment which deal with the problem of applicant competency as "conservative" or even "racist" attempts to "blame the victim" for his or her misfortunes   (See Benokraitis and Feagin, 1978: 204-209). In some instances, these epithets have been well deserved. Nevertheless, the issue of applicant competency is a valid one; it cannot be dismissed as a racist red herring. The question is not whether many blacks are unable to compete effectively for jobs, but why are they unable to do so.

It would require a lengthy paper simply to catalogue the diverse explanations which have been given for this state of affairs. However, for our purposes, it would be useful to focus on two disparate and influential types of explanations: the first type of argument assumes that blacks compete in a truly free market, while the second argues that the ability of blacks to compete for jobs has been largely determined by the realities of the American social structure (Almquist, 1979; Rosenbloom, 1977; Swinton, 1983: 45-114; Wilson, 1980).

The free market explanation has its philosophical roots in classical liberalism and finds academic support in the discipline of American economics. Perhaps most importantly, it derives its plausibility from the fact that it is in accord with the conventional wisdom of the dominant American ideology. This theory argues that employers rationally choose employees on the basis of merit and productivity; any other course would entail a loss of profits or efficiency to the employer. The central task of job applicants is to prepare themselves for the jobs they seek. They are ultimately responsible for their own fates. Any tampering with this rational allocation of talent by the marketplace results in lower productivity not only for the employer, but for society as a whole.   Governmental intervention in this process, no matter how naively well-intentioned, ultimately hurts the beneficiaries of its actions, because as society grows poorer due to decreased productivity, the poor suffer most. Thus, not only should government refrain from regulating the employment practices of the private sector, but it should emulate the private sector in its own employment policies.   Government intervention would hurt everyone economically in the long-run, and would create moral rot in the short-run by depriving its wards of their initiative and sense of responsibility for their own lives.

In contrast to this market analysis of black employment, another school of scholars explains black unemployment and underemployment in terms of America's social realities. This line of reasoning is sociological in its logic and, by American standards, radical in its political implications. According to this argument, human problems can only be understood in their historical and societal contexts.   Thus, the fact that many blacks are ill-equipped to compete for decent jobs in a technologically sophisticated post-industrial society is explicable in terms of the American historical experience of racial exploitation. Not only did slavery and Jim Crow prevent blacks from economically competing with European-Americans in the past, but these practices created a societal reality which constrains many blacks from effectively competing for jobs in the present. The slave system prohibited black literacy and trained most blacks only for primitive field work. After the abolition of slavery, a century of Jim Crow practices denied the vast majority of black people equal educational and vocational opportunities.   In this racist social order, displays of black initiative were severely punished.   As a result of these practices, a black underclass exists which is imprisoned in urban and rural slums with inadequate housing, nutrition, schools, and police protection.   Many of the residents of these ghettos display the mental attitudes associated with a culture of poverty. Aggressive governmental action is required to solve the problems caused by past public and private racial oppression.   Governmental neutrality in the area of black employment is the moral equivalent of approving past racist crimes.   The absence of overt discrimination in the present cannot compensate for the sins committed in the past.

These two approaches differ as dramatically in their analyses of employer bias as they do in their assessments of the problem of applicant competency. To the market analyst, the employer is a rational actor attempting to locate the best qualified employees.   Employers welcome fair employment legislation, because it frees them from taking ascriptive factors into account in hiring decisions. However, any governmental interference with the employer's right to base this decision on achievement criteria, whether premised on Jim Crow or affirmative action criteria, is contrary to rational personnel procedures.

The sociological perspective, however, leads to a far more complex picture of the hiring process. First of all, in the real world bias does exist, and employers, left to their own devices, will often be guided by their own prejudices rather than utilitarian calculations when making hiring decisions. Second, the issue of "merit" is far more complex than the market analysts would have us believe. Notions of merit are culturally determined, and in the United States, job descriptions, pay scales, assumptions about qualifications, personnel tests, dress codes, and the like are all colored by cultural values which are clearly white, male, and Anglo in their biases. Finally, even if employers are free of racial bigotry or cultural biases, they will be ratifying the racist practices of the past by awarding jobs to those who are better qualified because of their superior environmental and educational backgrounds.

These sharply disparate perspectives lead to opposing conclusions regarding affirmative action policies. The market analysts favor passive nondiscrimination in employment and sometimes grudgingly accept programs promoting active nondiscrimination. However, they strongly oppose remedial employment policies, arguing that they are unconstitutional, immoral, and economically suicidal. In contrast, most proponents of the sociological perspective dismiss policies of passive and active nondiscrimination as woefully inadequate and assert that so-called reverse discrimination is simply the belated provision of social justice to peoples who have long been exploited. Furthermore, they argue that aggressive affirmative action programs are necessary to construct a truly nonracist, non-sexist society. Each of these points of view presents a normative argument which is compelling in terms of its own assumptions. The result is a philosophical impasse which cannot be resolved as long as the debate is over the extent to which affirmative action programs conform to normative ideals of social justice or liberal jurisprudence.

In my judgment, this intellectual deadlock can be broken by turning to an examination of the third factor relevant to black employment, employment availability. In doing so, we place the hiring decision in the context of economic reality and can begin to determine if affirmative action is a politically realistic strategy for achieving substantive racial equality.

Once procedural racism has been outlawed, the number of jobs available in the economy has far more influence than either applicant competency or employer bias on whether or not black workers can find decent jobs. Furthermore, employment availability strongly affects public attitudes toward the issues of applicant competency and employer bias.[4] In a scarce job market, "merit" and "experience" become prized values. Job applicants lack the power and employers see no reason to question traditional personnel policies. As the struggle for employment intensifies, generosity and tolerance disappear, and no one wants to pay the price for racial progress. Unemployed or underpaid whites may perceive black job gains as direct attacks on their own well-being. In this context, the awarding of jobs on the basis of race politically divides people into conflictive racial groups who had previously shared common economic needs and fears.

During periods of expanding employment, the logic of the zero-sum game disappears, and blacks can be hired without threatening the economic self-interest of whites. If a labor shortage develops, the issues of employee competency and employer bias become surprisingly easy of solution, as employers become more creative in the provision of job-training programs and much more self-critical regarding their assumptions about worker qualifications. The cruel irony of this situation is that in eras of economic depression and recession when blacks need affirmative action the most, they are politically least able to forge the political coalitions necessary to achieve it, while during periods of economic expansion when affirmative action programs are least needed, it is far easier to gain their adoption and implementation.

I believe an examination of American economic history substantiates my conclusions. During the wars of this century, when labor shortages appeared in both the private and public sectors of the economy, industrial, governmental, and military leaders recruited blacks for positions which had previously been closed to them. World War I led to the curtailment of European immigration and an American industrial boom. In egoistic response to their labor needs, northern industrialists hired thousands of southern blacks. World War II, the Korean War, and the Vietnam War brought about dramatic advances in black employment; it was only during these wars that the income gap between whites and blacks significantly narrowed (Weitzman, 1970: 3). However, during the economic stagnancy of the 1970s and early 1980s, and despite the enactment of civil rights laws, Great Society programs, and affirmative action policies, the median black family income (as measured in constant dollars) fell both in absolute term and as a percentage of white income (Swinton, 1983: 92-93). In this period, black unemployment steadily grew, so that today black unemployment is at the level of white unemployment during the Great Depression.

Furthermore, during the past decade, economic inequalities within the black community have increased (Swinton, 1983: 94-95). While it is hard to assess the impact of affirmative action programs on these developments, it is clear that they were unable to prevent this deterioration in the economic conditions of most black Americans, and it is possible that they may have aided most those blacks least in need of help (See Wilson, 1980). While many educated blacks have achieved positions previously denied them, the misery of the black poor continues to grow.

In emphasizing the centrality of macroeconomic factors, I am not suggesting that the fate of black workers should be determined by the impersonal workings of the marketplace. This approach imputes a benevolence to the market which it lacks. Nevertheless, many Americans feel that policies of "benign neglect" will solve the problem of black underemployment because they believe that earlier generations of poor European immigrants were able to enter the American mainstream without government help. It is a historical fact that millions of European workers entered the American economy during periods of rapid economic expansion when a strong demand existed for unskilled labor. The descendants of these workers have become members of the American middle class. However, this experience does not provide support for a laissez-faire solution to black poverty, because it ignores two important realities: (1) White-ethnic Americans have benefitted substantially from the government's intervention in the economy during the past half-century; and (2) their historical experience has no relevance to the current realities of and future prospect for black employment.

The Europeans who came to the United States before World War I entered a rapidly expanding economy at a time when unskilled factory jobs provided an avenue for social mobility. Their children and grandchildren benefitted immeasurably from government programs and policies established during the New Deal and World War II. The immigrant strategy of assimilation and upward mobility is unavailable to most members of the black underclass because of the structural changes which have occurred in the American economy since World War II. Poor, uneducated blacks are trapped in poverty by the fact that the labor requirements of a post-industrial economy experiencing slow growth are qualitatively and quantitatively different from those of the rapidly expanding industrial economy of the late nineteenth and early twentieth centuries (Wilson, 1980; Lieberson, 1980; Steinberg, 1981).

What, then, is to be done? If the preceding analysis has been correct, a successful strategy for achieving the fuller

utilization of black labor in the American economy entails a
two-level assault on the problem of black poverty: The first
level is microeconomic and focuses on the employer's hiring
decision; the second is macroeconomic and deals with the
problem of employment availability. My approach is pragmatic;
I believe that it is in accord with American political and
economic realities.

If the black poor are ever to enter the American
mainstream, federal and state governments must prohibit racist
employment practices, and this action must go beyond simply
requiring passive nondiscrimination in hiring. Active
nondiscrimination should be encouraged and rewarded, leading to
a fundamental revamping of personnel policies. Hiring, testing,
and evaluation procedures need to be reassessed, so that
realistic minimal qualifications for positions are determined
which are not culturally biased. Firms and governmental
agencies which have systematically discriminated against blacks
in the recent past should be forced to make restitution by giving
preference to qualified black applicants.[5] Personnel decisions
will have to be monitored to make sure racial discrimination has
ceased.

In pursuing these policies of active and restitutional
nondiscrimination, the principle of racial equality must remain
sacrosanct. (See Fullenwider, 1980; Goldman, 1979; Livingston,
1979; Foster and Segers, 1983.)[6] This principle means that if an
employer has not been guilty of racial discrimination in the
recent past, less qualified applicants should not be given
positions solely on the basis of race. In saying this, I am not
implying that reverse discrimination is either illegal or
immoral. If one has any sensitivity to the black historical
experience, it is difficult to critique reverse discrimination on
moral grounds. What I am asserting is that reverse
discrimination is a politically suicidal goal for blacks to pursue
and contrary to their own long-term interests. A fragile and
hard-won consensus currently exists on fair employment
practices. It is more in the interests of blacks than any other
group to oppose the institutionalization of racial considerations
in hiring decisions.

Reverse discrimination is an inappropriate strategy for
dealing with the problem of substantive racism, because it: (1)
patronizes blacks and gives credence to theories of racial
inequality; (2) aids those blacks least in need of help while
ignoring the suffering of the black underclass; (3) divides job
applicants along racial lines, isolating blacks politically; and (4)
is doomed to failure given the political and racial demographic
realities of American society. At best, policies of reverse
discrimination would destroy any hope of constructing a political
coalition which will lead to an improvement in the black

economic condition. At worst, they would fan the flames of an ugly racist backlash.

As I have indicated above, even the most aggressive assaults on racial discrimination in hiring will have only a limited effect on the problems of black poverty and under-employment. One of the key problems today is that there are not enough decent jobs available. As a result, poor blacks and poor whites compete for the scarce employment opportunities which do exist. This state of affairs can only be remedied by the creation of an electoral majority which will elect a government committed to the achievement of a full-employment economy and the elimination of poverty in the United States. Change in the direction of federal policy can only be brought about through the construction of interracial coalitions based on mutual economic self-interest. Interracial conflict must give way to intraclass alliances, and close attention must be paid to the mundane realities of conventional politics. Only progressive macroeconomic public policies can eliminate substantive racism in the United States.

NOTES

[1]Useful introductions to this controversy are provided by Barry R. Gross, ed., Reverse Discrimination (Buffalo: Prometheus Books, 1977); and William T. Blackstone and Robert D. Heslep, eds. Social Justice and Preferential Treatment (Athens: University of Georgia Press, 1977).

[2]An excellent explication of this concept appears in James M. Jones' Prejudice and Racism (Reading: Addison-Wesley, 1972).

[3]My distinction between procedural and substantive racism owes much to the arguments presented in the aforementioned studies.

[4]While these observations may seem obvious, they have often eluded many of the participants in the debate over affirmative action.

[5]I include the phrase "in the recent past," because I believe that it is politically necessary for there to be a statute of limitations for the crime of racial discrimination.

[6]My understanding of the philosophical questions raised by the issue of reverse discrimination has been greatly enhanced by the aforementioned studies.

REFERENCES

Almquist, Elizabeth McTaggart. 1978. Minorities, Gender and
  Work. Lexington: Lexington Books.

Benokraitis, Nijole V and Joe R. Feagin. 1978. Affirmative
  Action and Equal Opportunity: Action, Inaction, Reaction.
  Boulder, CO: Westview Press.

Blackstone, William T. and Robert D. Heslep. 1977. Eds. Social
  Justice and Preferential Treatment. Athens, GA:
  University of Georgia Press.

Carmichael, Stokeley and Charles V. Hamilton. 1967. Black
  Power: The Politics of Liberation in America. New York:
  Random House.

Foster, James and Marcy C. Segers. 1983. Elusive Equality:
  Liberalism, Affirmative Action, and Social Change in
  America. Port Washington: Associates Faculty Press.

Fullenwider, Robert K. 1980. The Reverse Discrimination
  Controversy: A Moral and Legal Analysis. Totowa: Rowman
  and Littlefield.

Goldman, Alan H. 1979. Justice and Reverse Discrimination.
  Princeton, NJ: Princeton University Press.

Gross, Barry R. 1977. Ed. Reverse Discrimination. Buffalo,
  NY: Prometheus Books.

Jones, James. 1972 Prejudice and Racism. Reading: Addison
  Wesley.

Knowles, Louis and Kenneth Prewitt. Eds. 1969. Institutional
  Racism in America. Englewood Cliffs: Prentice-Hall.

Lieberson, Stanley L. 1981. A Piece of the Pie: Black and
  White Immigrants since 1880. Berkeley: University of
  California Press, 1980.

Livingston, John C. 1979. Fair Game? Inequality and
  Affirmative Action. San Francisco: Freeman.

Myrdal, Gunnar. 1944. An American Dilemma: The Negro
  Problem and Modern Democracy. New York: Harper &
  Row.

20 Affirmative Action

Sasseen, Robert F. 1979. "Affirmative Action and the Principle of Equality," The New Egalitarianism: Questions and Challenges. David Lewis Schaefer, ed. Port Washington: Kennikat Press.

Steinberger, Stephen. 1981. The Ethnic Myth: Race, Ethnicity, and Class in America. New York: Atheneum.

Weitzman, Murray S. 1970. Measures of Overlap of Income Distributions of White and Negro Families in the United States. Washington: Government Printing Office.

Wilson, William J. 1973. Power, Racism, and Privilege. New York: Macmillan.

_____. 1980. The Declining Significance of Race: Blacks and Changing American Institutions. Chicago: University of Chicago Press.

Winton, David H. 1983. "The Economic Status of the Black Population." The State of Black America, 1983. James D. Williams, ed. New York: National Urban League.

Jeffrey Prager

Merit and Qualifications: Contested Social Meanings and Their Impact on Affirmative Action

INTRODUCTION: AFFIRMATIVE ACTION AND STRATIFICATION BELIEFS*

The issues raised with respect to the constitutionality and morality of affirmative action programs are fundamental ones: they go to the heart of the American value system and, as a consequence, have produced, within the implementing institutions themselves, substantial discord and division. The issues involved provoke intensely felt sentiments and deeply rooted polarizations. The consequence is that efforts at implementation remain weak. In this chapter, I will argue that these value divisions help us better understand the strength of opposition to these programs and the ambiguity that surrounds current legal interpretation concerning their constitutionality.

In a previous paper (Prager 1982b), I suggested that one source of weak public support and legal ambivalence is the strength of an "individualistic" value-orientation in American society, undermining the premises of affirmative action. That orientation promotes greater concern for fairness between individuals than it does concern for equity between groups. In this paper, I want to suggest an additional, perhaps even more critical, aspect of dominant American beliefs that serves to inhibit support for these new policies. Affirmative action, in addition to raising the issue of the nature of the American commitment to equality, makes problematic the legitimacy of the stratification system by which awards and resources are allocated and distributed. It subjects to debate the fundamental

*I gratefully acknowledge support from the UCLA Academic Senate Research Fund and the research assistance of Geoffrey Gilbert-Hamerling.

procedures by which scarce goods are distributed fairly throughout the society: in short, the presence of these programs challenges the prevailing understanding of the true meaning of merit and qualifications; they challenge an American commitment to a meritocracy.

In a recent article, Kleugel and Smith (1982) argue that opposition to affirmative action, rather than being exclusively an expression of racial animosities, derives from a belief in the openness and legitimacy of the American stratification system. Those Americans who see their opportunity as "plentiful" and identify others' position in the stratification hierarchy as a function of individual talents and efforts, tend to reject the premises upon which affirmative action is built (Kluegel and Smith 1982:523). These individualistic understandings of the stratification system preclude a "structural" or social appreciation of the limits to black opportunity, identifying lower upward mobility for blacks as a function of individual attributes. A defense of affirmative action can only occur when there exists an appreciation of the nonindividualistic sources of the American stratification order.

How does this contest between understandings of the stratification system enter concretely into the affirmative action debate? How are the "individualistic" and "structuralistic" positions framed in public discourse such that the former position has emerged as decisively dominant while the latter argument fails to command substantial following? What are the features of this discourse "format"--the structure of the debate between the two sides--that prevent reconciliation between the sides and inhibit the emergence of a consensual understanding concerning public policy?

The mechanisms by which scarce resources are allocated in the society are typically understood through reference to the twin concepts of merit and qualifications. Determining rewards with respect to individual merit and appropriate qualifications is generally thought to be the procedure that best realizes the values of equity and justice. Typically, the term "merit" and the term "qualifications" are used interchangeably and treated synonomously. Both merit and qualifications are understood as attributes of an individual, ones that the rewarding institutions have an obligation to properly assess. They are seen as essential elements of commitment to a meritocracy.

Seen through this meritocratic frame of reference, the one concept of qualifications is synonomous with the other, merit. As a result, we commonly expect that the allocation of rewards--jobs, positions in a law school class, etc.--will be offered to those individuals most qualified. The most talented individual is properly first in line to receive the available rewards. Thus, to suggest that the criteria of admissions or hiring ought to be altered to accommodate racial minorities quickly produces the charge of "reverse discrimination."

Similarly, those who assert that the existing criteria are "culturally biased" and therefore should be ignored, criticize the application of universally-based standards, applicable to all individuals equally. Both of these positions presume the meritocracy, but one side embraces an individualized understanding of it and endorses the concept, while the other side sees it through "structural" lenses and rejects it. On the one side, the meritocracy stands as the hallmark of the democratic achievement in its aspiration to universality; on the other, it is a mechanism designed to insure that the racially privileged remain so.

And yet, despite this division, various institutions have been legally and legislatively mandated to implement policies promoting greater minority representation, while still maintaining the integrity of the institution and its admission, hiring or promotion criteria. Seeking to promote a form of affirmative action while not abandoning the meritocracy, institutional actors have been forced to chart their own terrain. They cannot be guided by an emergent public consensus for it is not forthcoming (Condran 1979:463, Burstein 1979, Prager 1982a); nor have they been able to follow the letter of the law for it is currently rife with ambiguity. Instead, institutions have been without firm moorings: the impulse has been to develop programs that satisfy, in some measure, confused legal-bureaucratic mandates while also making overtures to a polarized public increasingly skeptical of the legitimacy of these institutional practices (Cf. Freedman 1978:105-15). The challenge indeed has been profound: how to preserve a meritocratic order while accomplishing simultaneously competing social purposes.

MERIT AND THE DEMOCRATIC DILEMMA

In his essay on bureaucracy, Max Weber writes,

> "Democracy" also takes an ambivalent stand in the face of specialized examinations, as it does in the face of all phenomena of bureaucracy--although democracy itself promotes these developments. Special examinations, on the one hand, mean or appear to mean a "selection" of those who qualify from all social strata rather than a rule of notables. On the other hand, democracy fears that a merit system and educa-

> tional certificates will result in a
> privileged "caste." Hence, democracy
> fights against the special-examination
> system (1946:240).

Weber anticipates the contemporary debate over the meaning and assessment of merit that has been central to the affirmative action controversy. Special examinations, as Weber notes, were introduced into democractic-bureaucratic orders to protect the society from a "rule of notables." The development of these impersonal standards of evaluation represented a major accomplishment in strengthening the place of the individual in society and weakening the role of "non-meritorious" features in the stratification system (cf. Schudson, 1972). The ability of the individual to perform well on an examination would take precedence over all particularistic considerations in the allocation of rewards. Thus, one of the distinguishing features of a liberal democratic order is its identification of "individual merit" as the basis upon which the stratification system is constructed.

There is no denying the revolutionary achievement in developing these impersonal mechanisms for individual evaluation, especially when contrasted with pre-meritocratic orders. Yet the reliance on standardized tests for their objectivity denies the countervailing danger that Weber points to: namely, the development of a privileged "caste." Typically, the vocabulary of the meritocracy is employed today to oppose any measures that seek to combat the development of an elite whose privileged position is a consequence of unfair access to social rewards through the special-examination system.

In their celebration of the virtues of impersonality in evaluating merit, proponents of this view presume that each individual stands in equal relation to one another and to the available awards: the only distinction of consequence is that of individual ability. Operating like a free market, the meritocracy selects those individuals--anonymous except for their demonstrated performance--best suited to occupy the given positions of power and responsibility. Further, the impersonality of the free market mechanisms, like the invisible hand, will best benefit the nation at large. Ability is conceived as an essential feature of the individual: when ability is present, it will manifest itself regardless of external circumstances. Merit is viewed as lodged in the person and manifest regardless of situation. And it follows from the free market imagery that when the society attends solely to the issue of individual ability--when it ignores circumstance and social context-- the gains will be greatest to the society. Only excellence will be rewarded, irrespective of the more particularistic claims made upon the nation's institutions.

Because merit is identified as an essential possession of the individual, society is viewed as composed of individuals hierarchically arranged according to merit. As Antonin Scalia argues:

> Unfortunately, the world of employment applicants does not divide itself merely into "qualified" and "unqualified" individuals. There is a whole range of ability--from unqualified, through minimally qualified, qualified, well-qualified, to outstanding. If I can't get Leontyne Price to sing a concert I have scheduled, I may have to settle for Elma Glatt. La Glatt has a pretty good voice, but not as good as Price. Is she unqualified? Not really--she has sung other concerts with modest success. But she's just as not as good as Price. Any system that coerces me to hire her in preference to Price, because of her race, degrades the quality of my product and discriminates on racial grounds against Price (1979:149).

Scalia's comments reveal additional features of this "individualistic" greatest merit, while La Glatt, still talented, cannot compare to the best. Such an argument presumes, in addition to its individual and hierarchical character, that merit is a solitary and unidimensional "thing"--an attribute that all members of the society can in good faith, agree upon. In the same way that Scalia presumes that all members of the community share in his evaluation of Price, he further assumes that one solitary, consensually agreed upon attribute, like voice, intelligence, or beauty, can be identified for a given reward.

In the case of the special examination for higher education, intelligence is the single attribute which is being measured and valued. It is assumed, moreover, that intelligence accurately predicts success for the position being tested. "It is well known to the public," Scalia argues, "that the outstanding institutions of higher education graduate the best and the brightest principally through the simple device of admitting only the best and the brightest" (1979: 159). Chief Justice Hale, dissenting from an opinion in the Washington State Supreme Court, which judged a special admissions program at the University of Washington constitutional, argued that "the discriminatory action in refusing him (DeFunis) admission becomes even more glaring when an overall view is taken of the admission practices. Of the 275 students who were explicitly told they had been accepted to the entering 1971 fall class, 180 had lower junior and senior grade point averages than Plaintiff DeFunis and only 95 had higher" (DeFunis v. Odegaard, Wash. 507 P.29 (1973):1191).

From Justice Hale's point of view, the failure to admit DeFunis on the basis of his demonstrated superiority to most of the entering class on the basis of his GPA constitutes a violation of the individuality and impersonality of the meritocracy. It is possible, Hale argues, to measure merit in a single, quantifiable variable, and allocate positions accordingly. Hale insists, referring to the denial of admission to DeFunis, that "all of these inequities are, I fear, bound to foster a spirit of anti-intellectualism in the heart of what should be an intellectual center" (DeFunis v. Odegaard, Wash 507 P.29 (1973):1196). Thus, both Hale and Scalia agree that the sole criterion by which individuals ought to be admitted to law schools is on the basis of intellectual merit, and the measure of that is one's GPA and LSAT scores.

If merit stands as an essential attribute of the individual, it is hierarchically distributed from one individual to the next, and if its correspondence to specific social roles--e.g., singer, student, beauty queen--is commonly agreed upon, then any conception of affirmative action towards given social groups violates the spirit of the meritocracy. Affirmative action requires, therefore, a basic challenge to this dominant understanding of merit and a reconceptualization of the meaning of the meritocracy.

Earlier, I suggested that proponents of affirmative action require an appreciation of the structural limits to opportunity that mitigate against individual talent and effort. This "structuralism" with regard to merit is expressed through: 1) a rejection of the idea of a hierarchy of merit, 2) a broader conception that locates merit not in the individual per se but in an individual situated within a social community that values certain talents and not others, and 3) an understanding that no one-dimensional measure can adequately assess a person's merit.

Taken together, this newly emergent understanding of merit appreciates that individual talents and efforts cannot be understood outside of a social context that rewards certain particular strengths and diminishes others. Cunning, for example, is a talent differentiated among individuals; yet only in few instances is it rewarded in this society. Merit, in short, is hardly an absolute characterization of the individual but intimately connected to a social definition of what ought to be rewarded. If this position towards merit easily distinguishes this new view from a more traditional, individualistic understanding, a more difficult problem for those holding the former conception is whether race per se is a merit deserving of reward.

Except for a still weak "middle position" that I will discuss shortly, proponents of affirmative action have tended to dismiss traditional meritocratic concerns. The issue of individual merit has been replaced by a preeminent focus on racial diversity and representation. Rejecting the putative universalism of special-examinations, these spokesmen argue instead for race per se as a merit. And it is the assertion that racial group membership, at least in part, is a criterion of merit that has produced the substantial polarization over the affirmative action debate. Members of the court themselves, on a number of occasions, have contributed to this polarization process by rejecting the traditional individualistic commitments (Prager 1982b). In identifying race as a condition of merit, the aspiration for universalism and, indeed, for the meritocracy appear to have been abandoned.

Writing in dissent in the California State Supreme Court Bakke decision, Judge Tobriner illustrates how proponents of affirmative action are similarly susceptible to applying an absolute standard of merit. Yet, unlike the individualists, in this case the criterion is exclusively particularistic; namely, race. Tobriner writes, "given the race and ethnic background of the great majority of the students admitted by the medical schools, minority applicants possess a distinct qualification for medical school simply by virtue of their ability to enhance the diversity of the student body" (Bakke v. Regents of the University of California, 18 Cal. 3d. 34(1976):83).

In this rendering of the argument, race itself, or, more accurately, racial minority status, emerges as a meritorious feature of the individual. While attempting to be more sensitive to the realities of American structural inequality by rejecting a pure measure of "intelligence" as meriting reward, these proponents unwittingly replace intelligence with a similarly narrow standard of reward, i.e., ascriptive status. The argument is made, for example, that minorities admitted to law school today are fully qualified because their records exceed "the average levels for all applicants of fifteen years ago." Thus, admission by race is fully justified when it can safely be presumed that the "applicant could successfully complete the program of instruction and become a competent member of the bar" (Brief for Sanford H. Kadish, et al. as Amici Curiae, Regents of the University of California v. Bakke). With this line of argumentation there is little pretense to the preservation of a meritocracy: law schools should not understand themselves as attempting to produce the best and the brightest, as Scalia suggests, but, rather, to serve as a credentialing institution motivated by a concern for racial equity.

Karst and Horowitz (1974) make a compelling argument
for the broadening of the understanding of merit, consistent
with an appreciation of the societal context in which it
operates. "The principle that careers should be open to talent
is not primarily based on the justice of rewarding the
individual," they argue, "it is, above all, a principle based on a
perception of social needs" (1974:961).   And implicitly they
argue that if racial representation in law schools or the legal
profession is deemed a legitimate social need, then race is as
good a basis as any for determining social rewards.   All
classifications are socially constructed; they imply "a selection
of certain attributes as the relevant ones--the 'merits.' Once
this selection is made, an individual is classified either with
those who possess the relevant attributes or with those who do
not" (1974:959,962). Karst and Horowitz are undoubtedly right
in representing the relationship of merit to either implicit or
explicit notions of social need.   "Intelligence" is only a
reasonable merit for law school if the sole aim is to produce the
"best and the brightest." If, however, the social purposes of the
legal institution are multi-dimensional, as they surely are, then
the criteria for merit similarly have to respond to that multi-
dimensionality.

Yet in suggesting that classifications are all socially
constructed, Karst and Horowitz assert that any classification--
whether individualistic or particularistic--is equally legitimate.
They do not suggest criteria to distinguish between legitimate
and illegitimate classification. In the absence of such criteria,
we are left with only fluid political and social understandings.
The determination of social need can be made without reference
to more general principles and values.

This movement away from classical meritocratic
principles revolving around the individual in the interest of
racial diversity is made clearer in the assertion that
standardized exams are insufficient or inaccurate indicators of
merit. Justice Douglas of the U.S. Supreme Court argued, for
example, that "the traditional combination of LSAT and GPA
may have provided acceptable predictors of likely performance
in law school in the past. But there is no clear evidence that the
LSAT and GPA provide particularly good evaluations of the
intrinsic or enriched ability of an individual to perform as a law
student or lawyer in a functioning society undergoing change.
Nor is there any clear evidence that grades and other evaluators
of law school performance, and the bar examination, are
particularly good predictors of competence or success as a
lawyer" (DeFunis v. Odegaard 416 US 312 (1974):176; citing S. J.
Rosen, 1970:3221, 323-3).

There are confusing and contradictory parts to Douglas'
line of reasoning. But in this respect he is clear: the problem of

measuring merit is so acute by racial or cultural groups that different standards ought to be employed by group standing (DeFunis v. Odegaard 416 US 312 (1974):178). No single universal standard is possible by which to evaluate merit; society is forced to relativize the procedures by which merit is awarded.

These two sets of positions toward merit--one, individualistic, asociological and absolutist; the other, collectivistic, sociological and relativistic--reveal one pole around which the affirmative action debate turns. The former position is intensely argued because it is perceived as under attack by proponents of affirmative action, while the latter position is adhered to stridently because of the refusal by many to acknowledge the serious problem of racial underrepresentation.

In his decisive opinion in the Bakke case (Regents of the University of California v. Bakke 438 US 265 (1978)), Justice Powell attempts to relativize and sociologize merit while maintaining a commitment to a meritocracy based upon individual achievement. His goal is to provide a basis upon which a multi-dimensional, non-absolute set of evaluative criteria might be established to identify individuals possessing merit. Powell attempts, first, to move away from a completely hierarchical conception of meritocracy, asserting instead that the vast majority of applicants to, say, a law school are admissible and capable of doing good work. The challenge is to establish criteria of admissions which, while not violating the essential precepts of a meritocracy, prevent an elite "caste," e.g., those trained well in test-taking, from occupying the available slots. Thus, Powell asserts the criterion of "diversity," suggesting that a heterogeneous student body is a necessary component for talented individuals to be well-trained.

In contrast with Scalia's position that institutions produce the best and the brightest only by recruiting the best and brightest, this view suggests that individuals are affected by the educational environment in which they are trained. In citing the Harvard College Plan for special admissions, Powell argues:

> A farm boy from Idaho can bring something to Harvard College that a Bostonian cannot offer. Similarly, a black student can usually bring something that a white person cannot offer. The quality of the educational experience of all the students in Harvard College depends in part on these differences in the background and outlook these students bring with them.

(Regents of the University of California
v. Bakke 438 US 265 (1978):323).

In the interest of diversity, race can stand as one factor among many; the presumption being that a racial minority brings "something" to the class that otherwise would be lacking. In this rendition, minority status (like geographical diversity) is deemed meritorious, not because minority status per se makes the individual more worthy but that a minority individual would more likely enhance the education of the class as a whole. "The critical criteria," Powell insists, "are often individual qualities or experience not dependent upon race but sometimes associated with it" (Regents of the University of California v. Bakke, 438 US 265 (1978):324).

Merit is not an attribute that can be identified out of social context; it is a feature of the individual always in relation to the collectivity. If all applicants who applied to Harvard College had 800 SAT scores, they are not equally merited to attend. The fact that the purpose of the College is to provide a liberal arts education requires that, in the interest of the purposes of the College, other features in addition to performance on a standardized test be taken into account. Merit is viewed not as hierarchically arranged but, rather, as a function of the particular needs and purposes of the awarding institution. At the very least, merit is viewed as a distillate of attributes drawn from multiple scales. No one measure can absolutely assess merit but, rather, this "special something" is more ambiguous and amorphous. And, in contrast with a traditionalist understanding, "specialness" is a product of a variable collectivity with changing conceptions of what is important and with ever-changing ideas of the appropriate purposes of any given institution. In Powell's mind, an essential purpose of an educational institution may be to expose its students to the diversity of the nation; this criterion legitimates the use of race on an individualized basis. But the broader message of the Powell decision is that the determination of merit can not be accomplished independent of a conception of social purpose.

Powell's position has much to recommend it. In striking a balance between a concern for a meritocratic order, and an appreciation of a real social world that produces inequities between groups, he offers a way out of the contemporary impasse. And yet, the logic of his argument has been quickly dismissed because it spans two competing and distinct orientations concerning the meritocracy. While, in the abstract, Powell's position offers the possibility of bridging the divide between the two positions, its public reception thus far has weakened its potential significance (Cohen, 1980; Dworkin, 1978).

QUALIFICATIONS AND INSTITUTIONAL RESPONSIVENESS

Merit, as I have indicated, refers to attributes of the individual, subject to either an absolute, individualistic interpretation or a more socially relativistic one. Qualifications, in contrast, refer to a given set of standards that the institution deems appropriate and which they define. It, too, can be treated either as an absolute standard, for which only certain individuals clearly qualify or as a more relativistic criterion, where the discretionary role of the institution is more broadly appreciated. In either case, the institution serves as a gatekeeper in promoting a hierarchical and inegalitarian order-- it is faced with the task of establishing criteria by which limited positions are allocated to a few individuals. But the extent to which traditional meritocratic principles guide these hierarchical arrangements depends upon the particular understanding held of qualifications.

The debate over the meaning of qualifications reveals the dilemmas faced by institutional elites who often try to balance a narrow, "meritocratic" standard of necessary qualifications with a response to those who are critical of the institutions' illegitimate "exclusionary" character. Attempting to maintain their commitment to universalism while demonstrating concern for pressing social needs, various institutional elites have sought to forge a pragmatic response to the problem. Since the debate has tended to polarize public discourse, institutional elites have been attempting to reconcile countervailing pressures on the institutions.

The dominant and traditional understanding of qualification is one that imagines there to be a hierarchy of individuals, lined up in a row from "most qualified" to "least qualified." As Antonin Scalia asserted when speaking of professional singers, there is only one singer who stands unequally above others, and so on down the line. This imagery reflects a conception of institutions competing amongst themselves to serve the available "merited" individuals. If, for example, Leontyne Price stopped singing, then the second best available singer would become the "best." Institutions define qualifications not principally in terms of abstract criteria of what is required for excellent performance but, rather, in terms of the concrete individuals available who desire entry into that institution. Qualifications become, in short, defined in terms of the basic market principles of supply and demand.

The issue of qualification is different than that of merit for the following reason: while the understanding of individual attributes, i.e., merits, necessary for success may vary--e.g., intelligence, personality, motivation--the traditional under-standing of qualifications is one where those attributes are ordinarily distributed between individuals. The challenge of an institution is to identify those most "qualified" and successfully compete for them. Justice Hale, in his DeFunis dissent most simply captures the logic of this understanding. He writes, "since no more than 150 applicants were to be admitted, the admission of less qualified resulted in a denial of places to those otherwise qualified . . . . Not being a member of a preferred ethnic minority, he (DeFunis) found his place taken by others who not only possessed far lower credentials and qualifications but among whom were some who on the face of their records were unqualified" (DeFunis v. Odegaard, Wash. 507 P.29 (1973):1197).

The presence of affirmative action programs, particularly in professional training programs, immediately raises the specter of producing incompetent individuals. Stated differently, it is commonly assumed that changing standards is to lower them, thus enabling the entry of individuals into positions of responsibility who do not rightly belong. As James Nickel writes, in discussing the dilemmas of affirmative action from a jurisprudential perspective, "in the case of surgeons, professional athletics and airline pilots, small differences in competence can make a great difference, respectively, in lives saved, games won, or crashes averted, and hence the scope allowed to preferential policies should be more restricted" (1975:545).

Both kinds of arguments--those that argue for the hierarchy of qualified individuals and those that assert the need for professional competence--unequivocally presume that the given practices for determining excellence and rewarding entry are the appropriate and only accurate ones. Qualifications, like competence, are clearly known in this rendering; to diverge from these standards is to produce an inferior product or, at best, to sacrifice excellence for some other perhaps socially beneficial purpose. But by the same logic, to recognize that qualifications have dramatically become more rigorous over the years, commensurate with an increased demand and improved performance by individuals, is to acknowledge that those trained in the past, by today's standards, are incompetent in their professional capacities.

In short, this defense of qualifications is a defense of the free marketplace of individuals. The awarding institutions, in this case, possess free reign to select those individuals for reward without respect to "social interests" or any other countervailing claims on the institution. With more individuals performing better on those measures deemed necessary for a successful career in a specific profession, the definition of who is qualified becomes commensurately elevated.

This understanding, then, is an absolute one in the sense that the granting institution knows quality when it sees it and each individual is aligned discretely on the qualifications continuum. At the same time, paradoxically, the conception is relativistic in its dependence on the available pool of aspiring individuals in any given year. These views produce, in addition, a conviction regarding the appropriateness of the existing measures of individual merit determining the chances of his or her success. Setting standards by use of the special examination, the LSAT, is defended on the grounds that it distinguishes the superior from the inferior individual, regardless of social position. As one commentator expressed it, "perhaps the test is 'culturally biased,' but so also may be the law school program and the practice of law, in the sense that they call for skills and attitudes developed in the dominant culture" (Lavinsky, 1975:587).

Thus, in all respects, this view of qualifications identifies the institution as one capable of selecting those individuals best suited to perform specific professional roles. It establishes the standards to which individuals must conform; and yet, without recognizing it, in relying on explicit standards as a vehicle to establish entry into the institution, this view succeeds in depleting the institution of discretionary autonomy. Its only raison d'être is to serve that small group of individuals who aspire to enter and who, in any given year, are deemed qualified to do so. The institution can neither broaden the criteria upon which individuals are admitted, nor see itself as an agency of broader social purpose. Qualifications, in sum, are vulnerable to the particular composition of the existing population of aspiring entrants. In contrast to the common view that individuals are subject to the idiosyncracies and excessive demands placed on the institutions, this conception of qualification produces an institution without integrity, and at the mercy of its applicants.

Defense of affirmative action programs requires a different conception of the meaning of qualifications. Proponents of affirmative action emphasize instead the largely discretionary element (one that might be made explicit) that institutions possess in setting standards. They assert the "socially created" character of institutions, a function of human choice and particular commitments. Qualifications, therefore, are neither absolute nor do they reside in the aggregate of individuals; rather, they are selected by institutional elites and they express the character of the collective structure. The practices of selection that currently exist are not beyond reproach, for they reflect specific socially conditioned choices about reward, however conscious those choices may be to the gatekeepers.

In suggesting that qualifications are neither sacrosanct commitments to individual excellence nor beyond discretionary manipulation, this understanding challenges free market individualism. This "sociological" view of qualifications does not ignore or dismiss the problem of "standards." Rather, the argument hinges on the inextricable bonds between a definition of standards, the social purposes of the institution, and the available pool of candidates--connections which the individualistic orientation attempts to ignore.

In contrast with a conception of a hierarchy of qualified individuals, the understanding here is of a pool of candidates, only some of whom are qualified. Those in the pool deemed qualified are equally qualified: each has an equal likelihood to succeed. Those excluded are deemed unqualified. In this sense, there is an appreciation of the fact that qualifications represent a more-or-less absolute standard established by the institution concerning the minimally necessary criteria for success in the institution. This conception directly challenges the hierarchical one; qualifications inhere in the institution, not in individual applicants. In testimony by a law school dean entered before the U.S. Supreme Court, this perspective is well articulated:

> Dean: (While) we do not have a quota...we want a reasonable (minority) representation. We will go down to reach it if we can, without taking people who are unqualified in an absolute sense.
> Court: Of those who have made application to go to the law school, I am saying you are not taking the best qualified?
> Dean: In total?
> Court: In total.
> Dean: In using that definition, yes (cited in Douglas opinion, DeFunis v. Odegaard 416 US 312 (1974):326).

From this exchange, it is clear that the dean offered the Court a new meaning of qualifications: the school does not take the qualified "in total," but that those selected have a "reasonable probable likelihood of...succeeding." Guided by other criteria, e.g., racial representation, an institution is obligated to admit only those students who are likely to succeed, not necessarily to admit those that are "best" qualified. Seen in this way--from the vantage point of the institution rather than the individual applicants--all those admitted to the program are qualified. By definition, no individual admitted was deemed unqualified. Such an understanding of qualifications replaces the fluidity of the traditional understanding, where standards are a function of the pool of aspirants. In its place is the establishment of an absolute minimum standard, one defined by the institution, and one which each aspirant must exceed.

The pool of qualified, as distinct from the heirarchy of qualified, makes vivid the discretionary authority held by institutions. Since more applicants are qualified than can be admitted, the admitting institutions are faced with two sorts of questions: 1) what are the minimum acceptable standards necessary to maintain the integrity and purposes of the institution? and 2) what is the range of legitimate criteria by which equally qualified individuals can be differentiated? When the problem of selective admissions is approached from this angle, the role institutional elites play in making these decisions--whether they adhere to the traditional understanding or the newer one--becomes more evident. Moreover, these decisions and subsequent institutional practices produce profound social consequences: changing practices could help reduce fundamental social inequities. The problem of racial underrepresentation, in short, is not a problem that defies human agency; specific decisions that have been made with respect to hiring and admissions have produced a systematic pattern of racial inequality and new decisions could help undo that pattern.

When one considers the prevailing logic of admissions procedures, it is clear that employing the imagery of this hierarchy of qualified individuals has produced an extremely timid conception of both institutional discretion and autonomy. As David Leslie (1974) suggests, this traditional conception of qualifications has created an institutional elite unwilling to admit any but those whose chances of success are extremely high. The result is to enhance the privileges of those already privileged. The following diagram illustrates the possible decisions available to an elite and the different consequences that obtain as a result:

Figure I

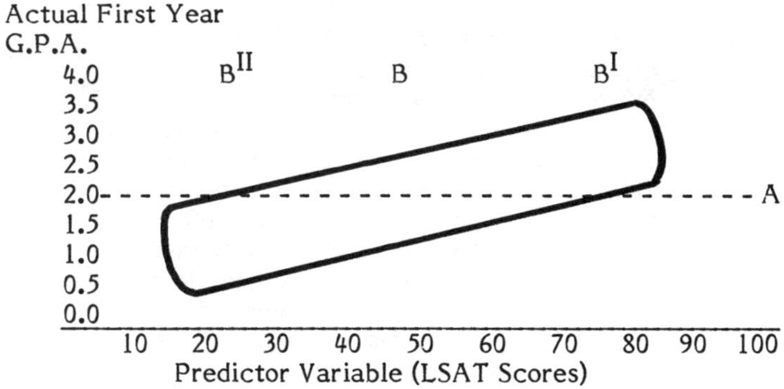

Actual First Year G.P.A. plotted against Predictor Variable (LSAT Scores), with points B^{II}, B, and B^I and line A.

A=Level of Acceptable Grades in Law School (2.0 is the traditional cut off, but this itself is arbitrary).

B^I=Level where the predictor variable shows 100% success rate (all of these students will graduate from the first-year program).

B^{II}=Level where no student will graduate from the first year program.

B=The Middle Mass. As one moves B to the right the probability of success increases. As one moves B to the left the probability of success decreases.

(Adapted from David Leslie, "Emerging Challenges to the Logic of Selective Admissions Procedures.")

        The diagram reveals, first, that the decision to accept the most merited individuals (B^I) excludes a wide range of applicants also capable of successfully completing the law school program. In perceiving itself as serving individuals, the institution restricts entry to all but those who, according to traditional criteria of success, are certain of success. When the perception shifts, however, to recognize that the institution has the capacity to perform a social service over and above training those individuals already most likely to succeed, the inclination may be to expand the pool of admittees and to employ other criteria by which entrance is granted. Here, the institutional elite recognize that since discretion is always a prominent feature of the admissions process, e.g., the decision to admit only the most merited, they can legitimately expand the criteria to include such things as racial diversity. As the U.S. Government argued in their amicus curiae for the Bakke case in the U. S. Supreme Court:

> The admissions process involves many difficult and subjective decisions. For example, admission committees often must consider whether grades from one college are comparable to those from another, or whether an applicant with higher grades should be admitted before one with greater self-discipline. Other pertinent considerations are no less subjective. Because admissions decisions involve comparisons of intangible qualifications, educational institutions

require wide latitude in making these
decisions (1978:27).

If this new notion of qualifications highlights the
subjectivity of institutional admitting practices, it has also
made more problematic the connection between the "predictors"
of success and the qualifications necessary to succeed in a given
institution. As the diagram indicates, because the largest group
of applicants is capable of succeeding, the problem of
distinguishing between candidates becomes more acute. While
the traditional understanding of qualifications, as we have seen,
is tautological--the level of individual achievement (LSAT, GPA,
etc.) defines the standards of the institution--the new meaning
insists that such measures of achievement may not correlate, at
least for certain groups of individuals, with the necessary
attributes for success in the school or for leadership in the
profession.

But this issue of the appropriate "predictors" of success
had often become confused with the issue of the appropriate
"meaning" of success. Once the argument is made explicit that
institutions in their practical activity exercise discretionary
authority, two questions about the legitimacy of their authority
quickly surface. First, the question arises as to whether
institutional actors employ the appropriate "predictors" of
success in determining who enters the institution. Is success
sufficiently predicated on performance on standardized tests
and grade-point averages? As the chairman of the Admissions
Committee at the University of Washington Law School noted in
his DeFunis testimony:

> We gauged the potential for outstanding
> performance in law school not only from
> the existence of high test scores and
> grade point averages, but also from
> careful analysis of recommendations,
> the quality of work in difficult
> analytical seminars, courses, and writing
> programs, the academic standards of the
> school attended by the applicant, the
> applicant's graduate work (if any), since
> graduation....An applicant's racial or
> ethnic background was considered as one
> factor in our general attempt to convert
> formal credentials into realistic
> predictors (DeFunis v. Odegaard, Wash.
> 507 P. 29 (1973):1174).

But a second question of institutional authority emerges as well. Proponents of affirmative action policies challenge institutions for employing a narrow and overly selective definition of the meaning of success for individuals admitted into the institution and the profession. Does success mean getting high grades in law school, passing the bar, being of service to a specific sector of the greater community following graduation, or distinguishing oneself as an exceptionally talented legal scholar? The fact is that the operant definition of success is no less arbitrary than the measures of individual achievement to determine who is originally admitted. The new understanding of qualifications has produced a broader conception of the meaning of success by those institutions promoting affirmative action programs. For example, the chairman of the Admissions Committee cited above reports that "in reviewing the files of applicants, the committee did ask the same fundamental question in every case: what is the relative probability of the individual succeeding in law school and making significant contributions to law school classes and the community at large?" (emphasis added) (DeFunis v. Odegaard, Wash. 507 P. 29 (1973):1186). The latter concerns constitute a new definition of the meaning of success in law school.

These questions of the predictors of success and the meaning of success have loomed much larger in institutional activity as a result of affirmative action advocacy. But predicting success and defining its meanings are two separate questions. Proponents of affirmative action, in their critique of current abuses of institutional authority, often collapse the two. The result, I suggest, is a weaker challenge to the traditional justification of institutional practices than otherwise might be made. Combining the two issues promotes a return to the more individualistic understanding of the meaning of qualifications, as defined by the pool of available "merited" individuals.

This confusion, in short, has inhibited the institutionalization of these new institutional procedures. Thus, the chairman of Washington Law School Admissions Committee, after defining the enlarged criteria of success employed by the law school, reports that "minority applicants were directly compared to one another under this test (i.e., making significant contributions to law school classes and the community at large), but were not compared to nonminority applicants" (DeFunis v. Odegaard, Wash. 507 P. 29 (1973): 1186). In this case, the difficulty of measuring minority applicants' past achievements as predictors of success was confused with applying a distinctly different standard of success for the minority applicant. The expectation that minority members may make a particular contribution to a class or to the community at large cannot stand as a measure of their probable success in the law school class. This conflation legitimates a movement away from "objective" standards applied universally to all students, and, therefore, marks a more radical departure from pre-existing institutional practices.

The Washington State Supreme Court itself is guilty of confusing these two distinct dimensions of the problem. They argue:

> The question thus raised is whether, in selecting those applicants most likely to make significant contributions to law school classes and to the community at large, it is arbitrary and capricious for the admissions committee to consider race as a factor in admitting qualified minority applicants whose strict academic credentials yield a lower PFYA (probable first year average) than that of some nonminority applicants who are not admitted. The answer depends on whether race is relevant to the goals of the law school admission program as stated in the guide for applicants (DeFunis v. Odegaard, Wash. 507 P. 29 (1973): 1186).

While the Court is careful to acknowledge that race itself does not serve as a criterion of merit, the separate issues of predicting success in minority candidates and the nature of the purposes of the social institution, e.g., to educate the best and the brightest or to promote racial diversity in the legal school or profession, are not disentangled.

Justice Douglas, in the DeFunis decision, demonstrates the confusion involved in both recognizing the salience that racial membership plays in this society and attempting to adhere to a universalistic and individualistic ethos. Douglas argues that "the key to the problem is consideration of such applicants in a racially neutral way. Abolition of the LSAT would be a start. The invention of substitute tests might be made to get a measure of an applicant's cultural background, perception, ability to analyze, and his or her relation to groups. They are highly subjective, but unlike the LSAT they are not concealed, but in the open" (DeFunis v. Odegaard, 416 US 312 (1974):380).

Acknowledging the difficulty of evaluating a racially diverse population, Justice Douglas argues for the abandonment of attempts at objectivity. Standards represent, for him, a mechanism to deprive certain racially underrepresented groups access to various social institutions. Therefore, the pretense of

objectivity should give way to a subjectivist approach to evaluation. While certainly an extreme argument, it reveals the dan-
gerous underside of institutions that self-consciously acknowledge their discretionary authority, that recognize their capacity
to realize social change, and that are aware of the substantial
subjectivity that inevitably infuses all domains of social life.
Possessing such consciousness, the danger is there, as Douglas'
position demonstrates, to yield to a defense of radical subjec-
tivism and forgo further attempts at universalistic objectivity.

Institutions too responsive to collective purposes, like
racial diversity, run the risk of abandoning efforts to find a
single standard or standards to which all individuals must comply. In responding to a pressing social problem, they forgo those
procedures necessary to secure a continued legitimacy on behalf
of the public; they ignore the danger of being popularly viewed
as subjective, arbitrary and capricious. If the meaning of
success has been broadened, it should be applied to all
students. Similarly, if the criteria of admissions rely more
heavily on "subjective" assessment, no individual ought to be
excluded from such consideration. In failing to assert a
rationale for measuring probable success or a standard of
success that is applied equally to all individuals, these
institutional elites are helping insure that programs of affirmative action will fail to command broad-based popular support.

With respect to the problem of qualifications, the two
positions offered, like the debate over merits, similarly reveal
the individualist/structuralist tension in American public life.
The traditional understanding tends to ignore the problem of
racial underrepresentation or other problems systematically
besetting specific groups in the society. It promotes, instead, a
conception of institutions that serve only individuals in a
completely universalistic sense.   In contrast, the new
understanding of qualifications is far more sensitive to the
collective problems facing America, is attuned to the role that
institutions play in promoting those problems, and is cognizant
of the capacity that these institutions hold for ameliorating
these problems. Yet, at the same time, their responsiveness to
current public issues, e.g., racial underrepresentation, and their
seeming willingness to forgo deep-rooted procedures of
universalism has insured the decline in popular legitimacy, and
weakened faith in the "objectivity" of social institutions.

No pronouncement comparable to that of Justice Powell's
on merit has emerged to integrate the new and old understanding of qualifications. There appears no clear way out of
the individualist/structuralist impasse with respect to qualifications and standards. While institutions have not, by and large,
abandoned concern for universal standards, confusion is
pronounced with respect to ways in which to enlarge and

enhance an institution's social purpose and discretionary authority while continuing to protect the individual aspirant seeking to gain admittance into that institution. It is not yet clear how institutions might further collectivist social goals, like racial diversity, without forgoing institutional standards that serve to demonstrate the predictability and objectivity of social institutions.

CONCLUSION: MERIT, QUALIFICATIONS AND INSTITUTIONAL LEGITIMACY

This discussion has attempted to explicate how issues central to American beliefs about the stratification system have, on the one side, promoted the creation of affirmative action programs while, on the other, prevented their broad-scale institutionalization. The individualistic bias in American thought--and the threat that affirmative action policies are seen to pose to this normative orientation--make nearly certain that the institutional resolve (and the legal and legislative one) to address problems of structural inequities will become more attenuated over time.

As I suggested, Justice Powell's decision represents, with respect to the issue of merit, a middle position, where a concern for group inequities need not mean an abandonment of interest in individual protections. But even that position has been embroiled in political controversy, being denounced, for example, as a mere "political compromise" with no coherent jurisprudential or moral rationale behind it (Dworkin, 1978). And with respect to the issues of standards and qualifications, confusion abounds. There has yet to emerge in public discourse a position, comparable to Powell's, that acknowledges the discretionary authority of institutions and, simultaneously, approaches the theoretical commitments to universalistic criteria in the allocation of social rewards. There are surely many factors that portend a weakening public commitment to affirmative action in the years ahead. But the persistent disjuncture between justifications for those policies and the rationale that lies behind the stratification order surely makes its own important contribution to this development.

REFERENCES

Burstein, Paul. 1979. "Public Opinion, Demonstrations and the Passage of Anti-discrimination Legislation." The Public Opinion Quarterly 43(Summer): 157-72.

Cohen, Carl. 1980. "Equality, Diversity and Good Faith." Wayne Law Review 26: 1261-80.

Condran, John. 1979. "Changes in White Attitudes Toward Blacks: 1963-1977." The Public Opinion Quarterly 43(Winter): 463-76.

Dworkin, Ronald. 1978. "The Bakke Decision: Did It Decide Anything?." The New York Review of Books August 17.

Freedman, James O. 1978. Crisis and Legitimacy. Cambridge: Cambridge University Press.

Karst, Kenneth and Harold Horowitz. 1974. "Affirmative Action and Equal Protection." Virginia Law Review 60: 955-74.

Kleugel, James and Eliot Smith. 1982. "Whites' Beliefs about Blacks' Opportunity." American Sociological Review 47(August): 518-31.

Lavinsky, Larry. 1975. "DeFunis v. Odegaard: The 'Non-Decision' with a Message." Columbia Law Review 75 (April): 520-33.

Leslie, David. 1974. "Emerging Challenges to the Logic of Selective Admissions Procedures." Journal of Law and Education 3(April): 203-20.

Nickel, James. 1975. "Preferential Policies in Hiring and Admissions: A Jurisprudential Approach." Columbia Law Review 75 (April): 534-58.

Prager, Jeffrey. 1982a. "American Racial Ideology as Collective Representation." Ethnic and Racial Studies 5(January): 99-119.

Prager, Jeffrey. 1982b. "Equal Opportunity and Affirmative Action: The Rise of New Social Understandings." Research in Law, Deviance and Social Control 4: 191-218, Greenwich, CT.: JAI Press.

Rosen, S. J. 1970. "Equalizing Access of Legal Education." University of Toledo Law Review 1970: 321-76.

Scalia, Antonin. 1979. "The Disease as Cure: In Order to Get Beyond Racism, We Must First Take Account of Race." Washington University Law Quarterly 1979: 147-57.

Weber, Max. 1946. "Bureaucracy," from <u>Max Weber: Essays in Sociology</u>, Gerth and Mills eds., New York: Oxford University Press.

LEGAL DOCUMENTS

<u>Allan Bakke v. The Regents of The University of California</u>, 18 Cal. 3rd 34 (1976)

<u>Marco DeFunis, Jr. v. Charles Odegaard</u>, Wash. 507 P. 29 (1973) 1169

<u>Marco DeFunis, Jr. v. Charles Odegaard</u>, 416 US 312 (1974)

Brief for Sanford H. Kadish, et al. as Amici Curiae, <u>The Regents of the University of California v. Allan Bakke</u>, 1978

<u>The Regents of the University of California v. Allan Bakke</u>, 438 US 265 1978

Brief for the United States as Amici Curiae, <u>The Regents of the University of California v. Allan Bakke</u>, 1978

W. R. Newell

Affirmative Action and the
Dilemmas of Liberalism

Professors Young and Prager are in agreement that affirmative action lacks a consensus of support in the American public, and that the debate over its merits and drawbacks has become increasingly polarized. Partisans on both sides at best talk past each other, at worse accuse one another of ignorance and bad faith. Not surprisingly, a debate of such intensity of feeling points to some underlying and historically deep-rooted questions about the character of the American regime. At bottom, it seems as if affirmative action in whatever version is difficult if not impossible to reconcile with traditional liberal individualism, whether in the sense of the ideal of "free enterprise" economics or in the broader sense of individual rights. Both authors share this concern, although they have different suggestions for responding to it. After examining their arguments, I will turn to the liberal tradition of political philosophy to consider how it might clarify the reasoning behind arguments for and against affirmative action. By considering the views of three representative liberal thinkers -- John Locke, Jean-Jacques Rousseau and John Rawls -- we may approach some home truths, not only about affirmative action but about liberal democracy itself.

I

Of the four possible meanings of affirmative action distinguished by Professor Young, the fourth, reverse discrimination, is the most controversial. The first two allow employers to police or exhort themselves; the third involves restitution to a specific, previously injured group. The fourth, though, would obligate employers to show preference for a minority on the grounds of a societal responsibility to make up

for previous, general discrimination. In the following analysis, I
assume that "affirmative action" includes all four meanings.

Professor Young argues that procedural racism has been
greatly reduced in America if not altogether eliminated, but
that substantive racism persists -- the factual consequences of
past procedural racism and the hidden prejudices of employers
who conform outwardly to the letter of the law. Until we get
rid of substantive racism, therefore, the job begun with outlawing procedural racism is not finished; indeed, it enjoys a kind
of posthumous victory. Citing Gunnar Myrdal's early work on
racial discrimination, Professor Young argues that Americans
tend to look no further than the abolition of procedural racism
because they see nothing wrong with economic inequality so long
as the equality of opportunity is legally secured. This
"ahistorical" and "individualistic" ideology forestalls serious
thinking about how the "structure" of the American economy
prevents disadvantaged minorities from practicing the legal
equality of opportunity in a meaningful way (p. 11). In my view,
this stems not only from an American proclivity to treat ethical
questions "in terms of intentions rather than consequences," as
the author suggests (p. 11). It also has to do with a proclivity to
view the substantive inequality of result as demonstrating and
legitimating in practice the formal or procedural equality of
opportunity. Rather than being discounted, in other words, the
consequences count rather heavily. I will enlarge upon this in
discussing Locke.

Two mutually exclusive views of affirmative action thus
emerge. In the "free market" explanation of the economy, based
on the tradition of liberal individualism, "employers rationally
choose employees on the basis of merit." Government intervention through programs like affirmative action, the argument
runs, makes the economy less efficient by interfering with its
self-correcting mechanisms. It deprives people of a sense of
responsibility for getting ahead while lessening society's overall
wealth. Professor Young is surely correct to point out that this
assumption of rationality on the part of employers conceals all
kinds of less efficient, but equally powerful motives for choosing
some people for jobs over others. Proponents of affirmative
action, on the other hand, take a "radical" view of American
society which stresses, for example, that blacks still suffer from
their historical membership in a "culture of poverty and
racism." Governmental neutrality in the area of black employment thus becomes "the moral equivalent of approving past
racist crimes" (pp. 12-14). Professor Young leads toward the
radical view, especially when it comes to the question of merit
which dominates many debates about affirmative action. He pro-
nounces all "notions of merit" to be "culturally determined." In
contemporary America, merit is dominated by "cultural values

which are clearly white, male and Anglo in their biases." To reward people who come from such a background thus amounts to "ratifying the racist practices of the past" (pp. 13-14).

Here is where I have a problem with Professor Young's argument. Merit is certainly not synonymous with white, male and Anglo biases. But does it follow from this that all merit is therefore culturally determined? Merit may be something other than, or more than, white Anglo biases while nonetheless being something real or capable of being agreed upon. To conclude from the obviously partial and restricted meaning of merit that prevails in contemporary society that all standards of merit are arbitrary is tantamount to throwing out the baby with the bath water. For if every standard of merit is the equivalent of a "bias," what standard of justice are we appealing to in wanting to override or modify the prevailing one? (I assume that we consider just action to be meritorious.) If we can be indignant about what Professor Young calls the "crimes" committed against blacks throughout American history, this must be because we believe we have access to a standard of justice which forbids such practices. If minorities deserve a chance for meaningful opportunity, this must be because opportunity contributes to a kind of life we recognize as a worthy choice. If, on the other hand, the desire for affirmative action represents nothing but the self-interest of the minorities involved, why should the entrenched majority yield its arbitrary biases in order to allow another, equally arbitrary set of biases to get ahead? Professor Prager, as we will see, is more persuasive on the problem of how to define merit.

Professor Young does not think that the normative arguments for and against affirmative action can be resolved in any case. He urges us to turn from this "philosophical impasse" to "economic reality," wherein a practical solution lies. The solution can be characterized as a social democratic one, a sort of revivified New Deal. It envisions a full-employment economy, an electoral majority forged from "intraclass alliances," and "the elimination of poverty." He of course does not expect the blind workings of the market to achieve these things, but sees government as playing an active role in generating economic prosperity and opportunity. This would include vigorously implementing the various kinds of affirmative action except for reverse discrimination (pp. 17-18).

One must wonder if this does not reopen the question of the normative justification for these measures, a controversy which Professor Young hopes to preclude through his economic strategy. For it is certainly possible to envision a New Deal-style of economic management, including the stimulation of a full employment economy and the redistribution of purchasing power, without affirmative action. Professor Young excludes reverse discrimination on the grounds that it "patronizes" blacks, ignores the poorest blacks and exacerbates racial tension. He warns: "It is more in the interests of blacks than any other group to oppose the institutionalization of racial considerations in hiring decisions." I agree with this, but not on the grounds stated. For if the revivified New Deal solution begs the question of the justification for affirmative action, then the normative debate reopens. If reverse discrimination is just, one might argue, it should be undertaken regardless of its inexpediency. In any event, a strategy for slow, evolutionary implementation which would smooth ruffled feathers and get people used to the change could certainly be imagined, thus overcoming the objection based on inexpediency.

The core of Professor Young's position, though, is that this normative conflict will be dissipated once economic expansion really takes hold. Though he rejects the most narrowly individualistic and laissez-faire version of liberalism, his own solution shares a familiar liberal assumption that prosperity is the cure for all kinds of dissatisfaction and animosity. During periods of expanding economic opportunity, he argues, people are more generous and "willing to pay the price for racial progress" because they are less fearful of losing their own piece of a shrinking pie (pp. 15-17). I liken this to New Deal thinking because it shares the notion that governments can act positively, not to dismantle capitalism, but to regenerate it and redistribute its opportunities and rewards more equitably without abandoning the fundamental liberal faith in the individual's pursuit of his or her piece of the pie. This peculiarly American hybrid can make use of conflicting liberal or social democratic measures as the situation demands, and without the embarrassment of self-contradiction, because the resulting prosperity obscures differences in principle by removing the motives people have for entertaining them. A rising tide, as the saying goes, will raise all boats.

II

When he cites Max Weber, Professor Prager brings us to the core of the problem within the liberal tradition (pp. 21-22). Although liberal democracy establishes the equality of opportunity -- the "career open to talent" which was a proud maxim of the Enlightenment -- this can lead to a privileged "caste" which might eventually replace the pre-democratic rule of hereditary "notables." This points to the ambivalence of liberalism altogether: The equality of opportunity generates an inequality of result which limits the equality of opportunity. Which should be safeguarded -- the results or the opportunity? If we do not share Professor Young's view that this conflict can be washed away by the rising tide of prosperity, it must be resolved somehow in principle, as Professor Prager tries to do.

The problem with contemporary definitions of merit, he argues, is that they are made on the analogy of the free-market economy. This " 'individualistic' value orientation blinds us to an appreciation of the structural or social limitations placed on minority opportunity"(pp. 21-22). Merit is seen as a "solitary and unidimensional 'thing'--an attribute that all members of the Society can in good faith agree upon" (pp. 24-25). As with Adam Smith's famous principle of the hidden hand, it is to everybody's advantage, in this view, that an individual 'producer' of merit earn his or her reward. Society allocates power and responsibility to the best people; society as a whole benefits from being well-run. The assumption that an impersonal and objective meritocracy allocates rewards and status is so deeply entrenched, Professor Prager argues, that both sides of the debate over affirmative action accept it. Proponents of affirmative action, instead of seeing the prevailing definition of merit as flawed, believe they have to reject any notion of a universal standard in order to promote minority opportunity. In so doing, he believes, they concede too much to the other side (p. 23).

As a corrective to the traditional view, Professor Prager argues that merit cannot be defined "outside of a social context that rewards certain particular strengths and diminishes others" (p. 26). Merit, in other words, has to be seen sociologically or contextually, not as residing "in the individual per se." In particular, institutions should view merit as being inextricable from their own "social purposes." Universities, for instance, need not see themselves as obligated to reward merit solely as it is measured by test scores, but should use their autonomy to promote diversity for the sake of their educational ideals and to contribute to the societal goal of reducing racial inequality. This involves transforming the meaning of merit from a ranked hierarchy of test scores into a base line qualification whereby everyone admitted possess the "minimally necessary criteria for success." Everyone admitted will be competent. Beyond this minimum, Prager argues, institutions are not required to rank merit hierarchically by scores. Thus, racial diversity, for instance, can go into an expanded definition of what people contribute to an institution (pp. 26-30, 31-38).

Professor Prager hopes in this way to avoid the dilemma of choosing between an overly-restrictive view of merit or an idea of minority representation that casts merit aside. He is certainly right to suggest that the justice of affirmative action cannot be considered apart from the question of its standard of merit without demoralizing its beneficiaries and infuriating those whom it may displace. Thus, he criticizes proponents of affirmative action like Judge Tobriner in the California Supreme Court <u>Bakke</u> decision for treating race <u>per se</u> as meritorious (p. 27). This is just as narrow, he argues, as the traditional individualism. It merely replaces the definition of merit as the attribute of an individual with one in which it is the attribute of a group. Prager views himself as developing a theoretical framework for the sound common sense displayed in Justice Powell's decision on <u>Bakke</u> for the U. S. Supreme Court. Here, race is not seen as an "absolute" standard, but as one part of a mix from which the student body as a whole -- collectively and individually -- benefits.

> In this rendition, minority status (like geographical diversity) is deemed meritorious, not because minority status <u>per se</u> makes the individual more worthy, but that a minority individual would more likely enhance the education of the class <u>as a whole</u> (p. 30).

Professor Prager's argument has many attractive qualities, but in my view it also contains some difficulties. For instance, he argues as if 1) the contextual definition of merit and 2) the notion that merit cannot be adequately assessed by a "one-dimensional standard" entails 3) the "rejection of the idea of a hierarchy of merits" (p. 26). Surely this does not follow, and would not be possible no matter how broadly merit was defined. The base line qualification set by an institution would still exclude some people as being less deserving than those who get accepted, if not on grounds of test scores then on grounds of not being "diverse" enough with respect to ethnicity, background, place of origin or whatever. Whenever one person is accepted and another is turned down for a coveted opportunity, and the decision is not simply whimsical, a hierarchy of merits is at work.

Similarly, it does not necessarily follow from the fact that merit cannot be measured by a "single" or "one-dimensional" standard that "society is forced to relativize the procedures by which merit is awarded" (p. 29). In order to challenge the narrow view of merit, Professor Prager need not have gone beyond arguing that no single quality or criterion of measurement unambiguously entitles us to rewards and status. There could still be a cluster of principles, or a multi-dimensional principle, that takes account of the diverse contributions people make. One could also argue that human qualities which all would agree are objectively superior -- say, the mathematical genius of Einstein or Hegel's philosophical ability -- are neither sufficiently widespread nor sufficiently

necessary for performing most of the tasks that society rewards
to deny anyone an opportunity because they do not possess
them. However this may be, by needlessly relativizing his own
argument, it seems to me that Professor Prager also throws out
the baby with the bath water. He exposes himself to the same
difficulty as Professor Young: If everyone's view of what they
deserve is as relative as everyone else's, why should we be
concerned about those who have been dealt a poor hand in the
socio-economic shuffle? Why should we care about anyone's
thwarted opportunities?

There is another reason for this caveat more in keeping
with the practical issue at hand. In my view, the most
interesting part of Professor Prager's argument is that "rights"
inhere at least as much in institutions as in individuals. The
notion that institutions endow us with rights, or at least impart
content to our rights in their respective spheres of life, is what
we might term a corporatist one. It sounds as if institutions
following his view would function in a manner analogous to
consociational democracy: The universalism of individual rights
as recognized by such criteria for merit as test scores would be
mitigated by another kind of right, the proportional
representation of groups. But would not some extra principle of
help to the disadvantaged groups in particular be required in
order to distinguish this kind of group representation from the
kind that has, formally or informally, been practiced by
institutions all along? Universities, after all, have always taken
"diversity" into account. For instance, Ivy League colleges used
to recruit a disproportionate number of freshmen from a handful
of prep schools in the northeastern U.S. I do not see anything in
Professor Prager's argument that would harness the goal of
promoting "diversity" specifically to the goal of aiding
disadvantaged minorities.

III

Looked at from the perspective of political philosophy,
these arguments invite us to reflect on some far-reaching
questions. Are the rights of the individual reconcilable with
some broader conception of public or social justice? What
exactly are our rights as individuals, and whence do we receive
them -- from nature, from society, from institutions and
language? Reflecting on what our rights are or might be leads
to different possible conceptions of a legitimate society --
which rights ought to be promoted, which can be curtailed,
which inequalities if any must be tolerated. These are questions
to keep in mind as we turn to our three representative liberal
thinkers.

John Locke is probably the source of the master
assumptions of American political theory from the Founding

Fathers down to the present (Locke, 1965:chapters 1-3, 5,8-13, and 19; Hartz, 1955; and MacPherson, 1982). Lockean liberalism postulates the inalienable right of the individual to preserve his or her life. The first and most natural way in which human beings seek to preserve their lives is through the acquisition of property, which they make their own by "mixing" their labor with it. By labor, Locke means not merely physical exertion but a person's entire range of productive capacities, including intellectual ability and strength of character. Civil society, in order to be legitimate, must secure the right to property by enforcing contracts and protecting citizens from crime and fraud. But there can be no question of government taking it upon itself to level differences of wealth or assign fixed maximums or minimums. For Locke, the existing inequalities of property have a higher claim to legitimacy than the opportunity for new people to acquire property in the same measure that an individual who has acquired property is more naturally an individual than one who has not pursued that right as successfully. Property owners are the "rational and industrious," according to Locke, because they have been demonstrably successful at actualizing the rights of man. This does not mean that the unpropertied have no rights. They are entitled to the same protection of the laws and freedom from arbitrary authority as the propertied. They are free to hustle and move ahead. But their opportunity to acquire can never override the rights of the already-propertied to retain their status.

In my view, this is the kind of reasoning, conscious or unconscious, more or less diluted, behind most arguments against affirmative action. Locke posits the equality of opportunity in the "state of nature" so as to show, by an abstraction from the inequalities of result that exist in civil society, why and on what terms that inequality is in fact legitimate. This means that governments can never, on their own initiative and without the consent of the propertied, curtail an individual's property rights or, therefore, the social privileges that inevitably go along with them (for instance getting one's child into a good college). As for the unpropertied or less propertied, their rights are not violated so long as they have a bare chance to compete. This view of things is perfectly expressed by James Madison in the tenth Federalist paper. In a paraphrase of Locke's Treatise of Civil Government, Madison says that the "first object of government" is to protect the "unequal faculties" for the acquisition of "different degrees" of property. His readers are cautioned against confusing this notion of republican government with those who "rage for...an abolition of debts, for an equal division of property, or for any other improper or wicked project..." (Federalist Papers, 1961: 77-84).

In sum, there is little in Lockean liberalism that would favor affirmative action, least of all in its most controversial meaning as reverse discrimination. This is not simply because Lockean liberalism has no conception of the contextual or social meaning of merit. Though decidedly individualistic, Lockean liberalism has a precise and plausible account of how individual merit manifests itself socially in the form of the current distribution of wealth and status. Thus, as I suggested earlier, the consequences weigh rather heavily in vindicating the intention. The derivation of a right to possess more property than others from the equal right of everyone to acquire property is one of the great feats of intellectual history, and one that succeeding generations of Americans have found remarkably appealing. It is far from being an unassailable argument, but anyone hoping to counteract its influence will have to supply an equally plausible account of what kind of human fulfillment, what kind of moral and mental excellence, would result from a less individualistic (or at least less Lockean) conception of justice. There is, one should note, no absolute prohibition in Locke's thinking against a legislature undertaking a program like affirmative action, so long as that government is responsible to its (propertied) electors. It is conceivable from a Lockean viewpoint that government could carry out such a program so as to curtail potential social unrest and buttress the long-term stability of the existing order. But plainly Locke does not think it likely that governments will go in for actions of this kind, and there is no way in his view that they could be morally obligated to do so.

Now Locke, of course, was not the only stream from the Old World that fed the course of American political thought. We see that other influences were at work when we note Jefferson's crucial emendation of Locke's maxim that government exists to secure the individual's "life, liberty and the pursuit of property" into "life, liberty and the pursuit of happiness." The sentiment here is often taken to be Rousseauan, meant to ameliorate the more Scrooge-like tendencies of Lockeanism. Rousseau's On the Social Contract certainly presents the most coherently reasoned alternative variant of liberalism to that of Locke -- one which is distinctly more favorable to the reasoning behind affirmative action.

In order to consider this, let us look at the famous Rousseauan concept of the "general will" (Rousseau, 1978; Rousseau, 1964: 78-90; Pateman, 1980: 22-44). According to Rousseau, the general will is operative when each citizen wills laws that are universalizable. This means that I cannot will any law that will maximize my particular interests at the expense of others. Nor, on the other hand, can I will a law that would subordinate me to some other person or faction (even if self-interest, admiration or habits of veneration inclined me to do so). The purpose of the general will is to maximize equality while enabling each individual to overcome his or her most immediate selfish inclinations for the sake of the common good. The public and private serve each other, but with an emphasis on the public dimension.

If we put the idea of affirmative action through the Rousseauan conception of universalizability... the results are interesting. It is clear that affirmative action could never be willed by its own future beneficiaries, since that would constitute a particular rather than a universal good. For the very reason that he was so devoted to the unity of society as a whole, Rousseau was intolerant of subcultures and groups, which he tended to regard as mere aggregates of selfish individuals. It seems to me, however, that affirmative action could be willed by the whole political community on two grounds: 1) That all would agree to its desirability if they were ever to find themselves in the situation of its intended beneficiaries -- that is, as members of an under-privileged minority. And 2) that for the harmony of society as a whole, so that no group will feel alienated and that citizenship does not work as effectively for its members as for others.

The Social Contract is thus markedly more open to the idea of affirmative action than Lockean liberalism, and in a way that would seem to satisfy Professor Prager's well-taken point that an affirmative action program should not manifest itself as serving a "particularistic" interest, but rather as something from which everyone benefits, if not in the same way as its direct beneficiaries. There are several reasons for this difference between Rousseau and Locke. Unlike Locke, Rousseau does not regard the curtailment of private property rights as being incompatible with a legitimate political order. In other words, he can envision a situation in which the citizen of a healthy republic could wish this for himself and for everyone else similarly situated. While against the forcible leveling or collectivization of property, Rousseau believed that the occasional limitation of property rights might be necessary for the general will's successful operation, inasmuch as it would forestall conflict between the haves and have-nots and prevent ambitious leaders from buying the support of the wretched.

Rousseau can argue in this way because his notion of the individual's rights included several things that Locke's does not: 1) our freedom as citizens of a participatory republic, 2) our autonomy as the irreducible natural dignity of every human being, and 3) compassion toward our fellow men. The three elements work together politically, socially and psychologically: To be free, we must will the freedom of others with whom we sympathize. Although Rousseau also regards the possession of private property as a right, these three components of our freedom rank high above it. Rousseau understands us to have more of a right to freedom than we do to property, and more of an obligation to be compassionate to the disadvantaged than to respect the inequality of the result. Thus, wherever the inequality of property can be shown to threaten these higher freedoms, property must take last place among our rights -- not no place, but last place. Thus, it is possible at least in principle to envision a kind of individualism that would require the rough parity, if not the absolute equality, of condition.

IV

Let us turn, finally to John Rawls' A Theory of Justice, a work which is probably the most distinguished contemporary inheritor of the liberal tradition of social contract theory (Rawls, 1971). According to Rawls, in order to be "fair" -- to recognize that everyone possesses equal rights -- we must abstract ourselves into a hypothetical "original position" where we are stripped of whatever natural and socio-economic advantages we may really possess. This involves acting as if a "veil of ignorance" concealed from us the advantages that would normally enable us to come out ahead of others in the competition for wealth and status. Having subtracted these "accidental" or arbitrary advantages from our sense of what we deserve, we can reorient ourselves to society in such a way that we will press our own claims less single-mindedly and be more tolerant of the claims of others (Rawls, 1971: 12-18, 60-62, 136-137, 208-209).

Rawls clearly wishes to use the hypothesis of the original position -- his own version of the "state of nature" argument familiar from the social contract tradition -- to distinguish legitimate from illegitimate practices within civil society as it actually exists. Yet, the chasm between the contentless rights of the original position and society as we really experience it makes it difficult, in my view, to think through the practical implications of Rawls' arguments. Unlike Locke and Rousseau, Rawls believes that a just compact among individuals can be elaborated apart from any substantive assumptions about human psychology, desert and fulfillment, and apart from any specific understanding of the public good, including an optimal political, social and economic order (Rawls, 1971: 11, 16-17). Whereas Rousseau and Locke have fully elaborated conceptions of human nature and moral self-development, Rawls can fill the emptiness of his own 'natural man' only by returning to what he takes to be the prevailing ethos of existing liberal democracies. Thus, he argues, his theory only justifies what are already "our firmest convictions," the idea of "justice as fairness" that "we do in fact accept..." (Rawls, 1971: 20-21). For the earlier social contract theorists, human nature and the state of nature were terms of distinction from existing civil society, which might or might not satisfy their requirements. Rawls, by contrast, seems to conflate the original position with prevailing opinion, and only a certain interpretation of prevailing opinion at that. This makes it difficult to see what would become of his theory's validity were there to be some historical shift in what "we do in fact accept..."

How might the Rawlsian theory of justice apply to affirmative action? According to Rawls, a principle of justice to which all would agree in the original position is that:

> social and economic inequalities, for example, inequalities of wealth and authority, are just only if they result in compensating benefits for everyone, and in particular for the least advantaged members of society (Rawls, 1971: 14-15).

In keeping with this, Rawls maintains the need for an open-ended, renewable equality of opportunity. Every individual, he says, is entitled to the material and social goods necessary for pursuing a "plan of life" (Rawls, 1971: 62, 118-119, 407-416). These principles could certainly be thought to serve affirmative action. When I suggested earlier that Professor Prager's argument was not specifically enough directed toward the disadvantaged, I had them in mind. They point to a way of helping the least advantaged without yielding Professor Prager's point that people should be treated preferentially only on the grounds that everyone will in some sense benefit. Indeed, Rawls' theory of justice is specifically intended to combat the utilitarian principle of "maximum net gain," according to which some people may be badly treated or allowed to suffer if society as a whole benefits (Rawls, 1971: 20, 65, 176-179). The flaw in utilitarianism, Rawls believes, is that it allows some people to be used as means to achieve other people's ends, thus violating equal rights. Rawls, by contrast, does not envision his own principle as ever lessening an individual's basic liberty, even while it may be used to compensate "for the lesser worth" of some people's liberty (Rawls, 1971: 204-205). This would seem to imply that opportunities could be redistributed through programs like affirmative action in a way that would not rob anyone of a right but would help the disadvantaged to exercise their rights with the same scope and potential as the rest of society.

Still, there are difficulties with using Rawlsian principles to justify affirmative action. Rawls believes that we can alienate our socio-economic advantages without alienating our rights. But what exactly remains for an individual to claim as a right -- as a basis for entitlement and freedom from arbitrary treatment -- once all natural and socio-economic advantages have been stripped away? Because the Rawlsian conception of rights is so contentless, it is difficult to imagine just where preferential treatment would exceed the limits of justice as fairness and become an overriding of some people's rights on behalf of others. In practice, both a minority applicant and a non-minority applicant for one place in an institution might argue that admission to this institution was indispensable for the pursuit of a "plan of life." It would be difficult to choose between these claims on the basis of Rawls' theory. Moreover, granting that the socio-economic advantages which a non-minority applicant might bring to the competition do not 'belong' to him in the Lockean sense, does it follow that they should be transferred to someone else? (And if so, to whom and in what degree?) Proponents of affirmative action might invoke Rawls' principle that inequality should aid the least advantaged, but opponents of it might equally well invoke his strictures against the use of one person as a means to the end of another.

These objections might hold less weight if Rawls could supply a notion of community in which preferential treatment for the disadvantaged was plausibly seen as necessary for the well-being of the community as a whole. This is where Rousseau's argument seems to me to be superior. Rousseau, as we saw, has a way of linking not only individuals' self-interest but their moral self-development to a specific political, economic and psychological conception of the public good. Rawls, however, is at his least persuasive when attempting to show that his notion of rights is compatible with a sense of community in anything more than an instrumental sense. Rawls maintains there is "no reason why" his theory should not be compatible with a conception of community as something good in itself, but he does not show how it positively supports one. This makes the potential clash of rights arising from justice as fairness more glaring and difficult to adjudicate (Sandel, 1984: 66-97, 133-154).

The weakness of Rawls' conception of community can be traced back to the characteristics of the original position. For in excluding any psychological characteristics from the original position (Rawls, 1971: 121), Rawls also excludes any plausible reasons for thinking that human beings are capable of caring for anyone but themselves, caring about the quality of public justice, and their self-improvement through citizenship. The original position, Rawls says, is one of "mutual disinterest" regarding any substantive standard of justice or the good life (Rawls, 1971: 128). In excluding from the original position collective sentiments of loyalty, indignation and self-righteousness on the grounds that they contribute to prejudice (Rawls, 1971: 206-209, 212-219), Rawls underrates the fact that these same sentiments can also fuel popular movements of benevolence and reform. Where would abolitionism have been, for instance, without a certain amount of starchy contempt for the moral shortcomings of its adversaries?

Although Rawlsian 'natural man' has the capacity to choose a version of the good life and the rationality to devise means for pursuing it, he has no access in the original position to ways of determining what the good life might be and commending it to others (Rawls, 1971: 13-14, 128, 138-139, 206-209). Thus, it is difficult to know how this individual would agree to anything -- why, in particular, he would accept "justice as fairness" over unbridled egoism, let alone a way of treating others that would be primarily for their own good or the common good. This seems especially clear when Rawls sets for the five criteria that he believes any sound theory of justice must satisfy: It must be generalizable, universalizable, it must be publicly disseminated, it must oblige us to use it in preference to force and cunning, and it must override all other rules such as law, custom and social convention (Rawls, 1971: 131-136). Rawls concedes that egoism -- that is, being out for oneself whether it violates the rights of others or not -- is capable of being generalized, universalized, disseminated, and of overriding other rules. He prevents it from qualifying as a "theory" along with justice as fairness by claiming that egoism cannot obligate us. But this seems more of an assertion than a proof, begging the question of whether justice as fairness should obligate us any more or as much as egoism.[1]

V

How, then, does liberal political philosophy clarify the debate over affirmative action? Taking Locke, Rousseau and Rawls to be representatives of liberalism, we see that it is a complex and nuanced body of thought. Depending on which variant of it one stresses, it will turn out to be more or less favorable to government initiatives to extend or review the equality of opportunity. Still, one has to reckon with the fact that American political practice has always leaned more heavily toward the Lockean variant, the one least favorable to such initiatives. The American public's antipathy toward affirmative action thus has a formidable philosophical antecedent.

Even assuming that liberalism as a whole has more leeway for affirmative action than the Lockean variant, this is true only in a qualified sense. For, despite their different views of what constitutes the individual's rights, the thinkers we have examined share the assumption that the individual is logically and ontologically prior to the community. It is a fundamental premise of liberalism, in other words, that individuals constitute groups, and not the reverse. Thus it is very difficult within the framework of liberal principles to express the claim behind affirmative action as a group rights claim. It tends to come out instead as a special case of individual rights claims. This is clear from the reasoning of Rousseau and Rawls. Though they do not exclude an initiative like affirmative action, they see it as being universally applicable to any individual similarly situated. It must, at the level of principle, be color-blind, and, so to speak, group-blind. Translated into practice, affirmative action would have to be viewed as a temporary remedial measure for facilitating the equal opportunity of individuals who happen to be members of currently disadvantaged groups. Once the individuals have been satisfied, according to liberalism, their group consciousness will fade into the background where it properly belongs.

A political philosophy can never directly dictate political practice. However, since we live in a liberal democracy, we need to bring our policy decisions into at least some degree of compatibility with the principles of liberalism, if they are to command respect and hold up over the long run. I share Professor Prager's good opinion of Justice Powell's decision in the Bakke case because it was flexible enough to stretch the liberal understanding of merit to respond to a pressing social problem without abandoning the traditional liberal reluctance to grant groups or races the same status in principle as individuals. The difference between the acceptance of "diversity" and the acceptance of a racial quota may seem like a small one, but it is the difference between a conception of public justice compatible with liberalism and one that is not. It is on this ground that I agree with Professor Young's warning against the institutionalization of "racial considerations." Quotas can restrict as well as promote opportunity, as we know from their unsavory reputation in the days before affirmative action. We have no way of knowing what future uses could be made of racial distinctions once they were embedded in constitutional law. Considering the uses made of them in the past, the uncertainty alone should make us not want to see them embedded there. Powell's category of "diversity" may be something of an obfuscation, but it at least has the merit of being a liberal obfuscation.

It is interesting to realize, though, that even when a place for affirmative action can be found within liberalism, many problems remain. Should affirmative action have as its aim the induction of the most promising individuals from minorities into the mainstream of competition for affluence and status? Or should its aim be the advancement of groups as groups -- an aim which, contrary to the liberal tradition, tends to see membership in a group as being desirable in and of itself? This ambiguity goes back to the origins of affirmative action and to the debate within minorities as to whether their goal should be assimilation or enhancing the collective identity of a "people." Or is there some middle ground between these alternatives? Even if affirmative action were to enjoy a complete victory on the procedural front, these dilemmas of liberalism would persist.

NOTES

[1] Rawls writes as if "general egoism" -- everybody pursuing their own advantage regardless of the rights of others -- can only lead to reliance on force and cunning, and thus cannot be regarded as a conception of justice. But, as we know from Lucretius, certain kinds of egosim not only do not lead to a life based on force and cunning, but preclude it. And, as we know from Hobbes, a theory of justice is certainly conceivable on the basis of a psychology of egosim.

REFERENCES

Hartz, Louis. 1955. The Liberal Tradition. New York: Harcourt, Brace and World.

Locke, John. 1965. "The Second Treatise of Government." Two Treatises of Government. Peter Laslett, ed. New York: New American Library.

MacPherson, C. B. 1982. The Political Theory of Possessive Individualism, Hobbes to Locke. Oxford: Clarendon Press.

Pateman, Carole. 1980. Participation and Democratic Theory. Cambridge: Cambridge University Press.

Rawls, John. 1971. A Theory of Justice. Cambridge, MA: The Belknap Press.

Rossiter, Clinton, ed. 1961. The Federalist Papers. New York: New American Library.

Rousseau, Jean-Jacques. 1978. On the Social Contracts. Roger D. Masters, ed. and Judith R. Masters, Translated. New York: St. Martin's Press.

_____. 1964. "To the Republic of Geneva". The First and Second Discourses. Roger D. Masters, ed. and Judith R. Masters, Translated. New York: St. Martin's Press.

Sandel, Michael J. 1984. Liberalism and the Limits of Justice. Cambridge: Cambridge University Press.

Part II
Some Consequences of Equal Employment Legislation

Tom W. Rice
Kenneth Whitby

Racial Inequality in Unemployment:
The Effectiveness of the Civil Rights Act of 1964

Throughout the twenty years since the passage of the Civil Rights Act of 1964 social scientists have argued over its impact in diminishing discrimination between blacks and whites. The focus of much of this debate has been on whether black-white income inequalities have lessened. Many researchers have reported significant income gains for blacks relative to whites (Farley and Hermalin, 1972; Freeman, 1973; and Masters, 1975). Others stress caution, suggesting that at best black gains are slight and unequal (Bell, 1972; Glenn, 1969; McCrone and Hardy, 1978; Villemez and Wiswell, 1978; and Darity, 1982). Although examining income inequality is interesting and at first glance appears to be a relevant measure of discrimination, it suffers from two serious problems. First, the above studies use income data provided by the U.S. Department of Commerce's Current Population Reports which include as income governmental transfer payments.[1] Since proportionately more blacks receive these payments[2] and the amount of payments increased dramatically since 1964, this alone may account for a substantial portion of black income gains. Put differently, the lessened income inequalities since 1964 may in part be due to increased transfer payments rather than a relative increase in black earned income. Second, as Villemez and Wiswell show, most significant black income gains are "located in the higher strata of the black socioeconomic hierarchy" (1978: 1031). This suggests that black gains have been achieved at the cost of polarizing the distribution of black incomes. Villemez and Wiswell claim that if the current trend continues "it means that even on that far-distant day when black income equality (with whites) is officially achieved, most blacks will still be at the bottom of the ladder with only a relatively

61

small proportion of them near the top" (1978: 1032). This hardly seems what the framers of the Civil Rights Act had in mind as discrimination reduction. In short, these two problems call into question the results of the black-white income studies.

In light of the serious problems outlined above, it is somewhat surprising that income inequality has sustained the attention of so many scholars wishing to measure the impact of the 1964 Act on black-white discrimination. This is particularly true when a second measure of the impact is readily available, black and white unemployment rates. Unemployment is certainly as theoretically as sound a measure as income. Title VII of the Act, as well as calling for equal wages, prohibits employment discrimination. In addition, the unemployment portions of the Act have been policed by the Equal Employment Opportunity Commission just as have been the wage portions. Finally, the courts have interpreted the unemployment sections favorably toward blacks.[3] By using unemployment rates, then, the disadvantages associated with income are avoided.

Oddly, few systematic studies of the impact of the 1964 Civil Rights Act have used unemployment as the dependent variable. Economists have long utilized unemployment in studying the effects of the business cycle on blacks (Gilman, 1963; Becker, 1967; Thurow, 1969; and Smith and Holt, 1970), but social scientists have virtually ignored it as a means of determining the effects of civil rights policies. Exceptions amount to largely descriptive works which often compare unemployment rates over selected years without controlling for other influences on unemployment (see for example: Freeman, 1978). Those types of studies generally conclude that since 1964 black unemployment has improved relative to its white counterpart, but the lack of controls leaves the results questionable.

In this chapter we use black and white unemployment rates to gauge whether blacks have experienced gains relative to whites since the passage of the Civil Rights Act of 1964. We employ interrupted time-series analysis (ITS), which provides systematic estimates of the impact of the Act on unemployment inequalities between blacks and whites while controlling for other influences on unemployment.

MEASURES, METHODS, AND DATA

Since most of the studies on black-white income disparities use the ratio of black-to-white income as the dependent variable, it might seem reasonable to use the ratio of black-to-white unemployment for this analysis. However, we abandoned this ratio because it shows that black unemployment improves relative to white unemployment during economic downturns and worsens during upswings--just the opposite of the

conventional view. For instance, the economic slowdown from
1969 to 1970 saw white unemployment rates rise from 3.1 to 4.5
percent and black unemployment rate rise from 6.4 to 8.2
percent. Yet the ratio of black-to-white unemployment fell
from 2.06 to 1.82, indicating improving circumstances for
blacks. This occurs "because the percentage increase in the
unemployment rate for whites exceed(s) that for blacks" (Gilroy,
1975: 47). This is misleading because proportionately more
blacks became unemployed. "Blacks are then worse off relative
to whites even though the (ratio) decreased" (Gilroy, 1975: 47).
The same results are found in times of prosperity, except in
reverse. That is, the ratio of black-to-white unemployment
rises in good economic times even though the black
unemployment position may be improving relative to the white
position.

    This difficulty is easily corrected by using the absolute
difference between employment rates (Gilman, 1963: p. 92).
Using the 1969 and 1970 figures shows that the absolute
difference between black and white unemployment rates rose
from 3.3 to 3.7 (for 1969: 6.4 - 3.1 + 3.3; and for 1970: 8.2 - 4.5 +
3.7). This is consistent with the economic literature which
overwhelmingly argues that the black position deteriorates
relative to the white position in times of a slumping economy.
The absolute difference also works in reverse, showing black
gains during economic upswings. We use the difference between
black and white unemployment rates as our dependent variable.

    It is necessary to include in the ITS equation an
independent variable sensitive to general economic conditions.
Without such a control a decrease or increase in the
unemployment difference may just be due to a rise or slump in
the economy. A control is necessary, then, since we are
interested in unemployment inequalities between blacks and
whites holding the economy constant. We use the overall
unemployment rate as our control variable. It is widely used as
a measure of economic conditions and should be highly sensitive
to shifts in the dependent variable.

    We also include a second independent variable to control
for the effects of war on the economy. War usually acts as a
tremendous boom to the United States economy, thus lowering
the difference between black and white unemployment rates.
To control for the unique effects of war we have created a
dummy variable coded 0 for war years and 1 for non-war
years.[4] If war does have the expected independent effect on the
dependent variable then the coefficient for war should be
positive and significant.

    The ITS model used is outlined by Campbell and Cook
(1978: 223-224). For our initial equation, the ITS model consists
of three independent variables: 1) a counter for all years, 1 to N;

2) a dichotomous variable scored 0 for years prior to the interruption (1964 Act) and 1 for all years after the interruption; and 3) a counter for all years, scored 0 prior to the interruption and 1, 2, 3, . . . after the interruption. The coefficient for the first variable represents the dependent variable slope for the pre-Civil Rights Act years. The second coefficient registers the change in the difference at the interruption, and the coefficient for the third variable estimates the change in the slope after the interruption. To compute the post-Civil Rights Act slope the initial slope coefficient (ITS variable one) must be added to the coefficient measuring the change in the initial slope (ITS variable three).

The unemployment figures used were obtained from the U.S. Bureau of Labor's Statistics Bulletin series (a listing appears in Appendix A). Our study includes the years 1948 to 1983. Prior to 1948 a breakdown of racial unemployment rates is unavailable. Finally, since the Civil Rights Act did not become law until 1965, we use this year as our interruption.

FINDINGS

As is often the case when working with time-series data, regressing the three ITS variables and two controls on the black-white unemployment difference produced serious auto-correlation--a Durbin-Watson statistic of 1.51. To adjust for this we used Cochrane-Orcutt (CORC), a technique which uses an iterative procedure to obtain error term estimates equivalent to maximum likelihood estimators (Pindyck and Rubinfeld, 1981: 456-457). Table 1 reports the results when the ITS variables and control variables are regressed on the unemployment difference using CORC.

The summary statistics indicate the model performs well. With a Durbin-Watson statistic of 1.90 we can be sure the first order autocorrelation is corrected. The R-square reveals that almost three-quarters of the variance in the black-white difference is accounted for by the independent variables, and the estimated standard error is only .53.

Turning to the independent variables, we find that the first, the economic control variable (overall unemployment rate), is significant in the expected direction. Specifically, the coefficient states that as the overall unemployment rate increased one percent the difference between black and white unemployment rates increased, on average, .60 annually. In other words, for every percent increase in overall unemployment blacks became more than a half of a percent worse off relative to whites. Thus, as expected, in tough economic times, proportionately more blacks became unemployed. The second control variable, the war dummy, also behaves as anticipated. The t-statistic is very near significance at the .05 level and

Table 1.
The Civil Rights Act and Black-White
Unemployment Differences.

Variables	Coefficient	t-statistic
Economic Control	.60	5.71
War Control	.69	1.64
1948-1964 Slope	-.07	-.42
1965 Interruption	-.32	-.40
1965-1983 Slope	.25	1.25
Constant	2.05	

R^2 = .72   Standard Error = .53   Durbin-Watson = 1.90

coefficient means that in times of peace and black-white unemployment difference averaged .69 percent higher. So, unemployment inequalities do seem to be lessened during times of war.

The initial ITS variable, representing the pre-1965 slope of the unemployment difference, is far from significant, indicating that there was no appreciable trend in the difference over the 1948-1964 period. The 1965 interruption variable fails to reach significance as well, suggesting the Civil Rights Act had no clear immediate effect on the unemployment difference. This should come as no surprise since any positive effect of the Act would most likely be gradual, increasing over the years as enforcement budgets and efforts grew and as the courts ruled in favor of blacks in cases concerning the Act.

The final variable is the post-1965 slope trend. This is the key variable as it tells the direction of the black-white unemployment difference following the Act. Unexpectedly, the coefficient does not indicate a decrease in the difference trend. Instead, it reveals a slight increase, although this is statistically insignificant. This increase is calculated by adding the pre-1965 coefficient of -.07 to the post-1965 coefficient of .25. The resulting .18 hints that the black-white unemployment difference grew since the 1964 Act became law. In short, unemployment inequality between blacks and whites does not seem to have lessened since the passage of the Act, and may have actually crept upwards.

In an effort to further understand the disturbing post-1965 trend, we examined the residuals from the equation reported in Table 1. The pre-1965 residuals seemed randomly scattered about the predicted trend. The post-1965 residuals, however, were much more systematically arranged. The last seven years, 1977-1983, were generally above the predicted line, indicating blacks have been worse off relative to whites since 1977 than Table 1 suggests. The reverse was true of the 1965-1976 residuals. Put differently, the 1977-1983 unemployment rate differences were regularly underpredicted by Table 1, while the 1965-1976 differences were usually overpredicted.

This suggests that the Civil Rights Act may have been working as intended until the 1977-1983 period. To test for this possibility we added two ITS variables to Table 1. The first measures the change in the unemployment difference at the 1977 interruption, and is coded 0 through 1976 and 1 thereafter. The second captures the change in the slope for the 1977-1983 years, and is coded 0 through 1976 and 1, 2, 3 . . . after. The variable in Table 1 which measured the change in the slope after 1965 now taps the change in the 1965-1976 slope over the 1948-1964 slope.

Table 2 displays the results of this larger equation. The three ITS slope variables are all significant and convey some interesting information. The 1948-1964 slope coefficient states that prior to the Act the black-white unemployment rate difference increased at a pace of .11 annually. In the 12 years immediately following the passage of the Act this trend was reversed to a -.09 annual pace. This is calculated by adding the 1965-1976 slope of -.20 to the 1948-1964 slope of .11. Blacks, then, improved their employment position relative to whites during the 1965-1976 period, evidence that the Act was working as intended. Moreover, the rate of improvement, -.09 annually, is substantial. At that pace, unemployment rate equality between blacks and whites could be reached in as little as 25 years, depending on general economic conditions. This possibility, however, was shattered by the 1977-1983 period. This period's slope of .62, when summed with the other two slopes, indicates that the black-white unemployment difference increased at an alarming annual rate of .53 (.62 - .20 + .11). Without question, the black unemployment position relative to the white position worsened dramatically over the 1977-1983 years.

The remainder of Table 2 reveals the model is well specified. The two control variables are significant in the expected direction. As anticipated, the two interruption variables are not significant, indicating no sharp change in the black-white unemployment difference between either 1964 and 1965 or 1976 and 1977. The R-square is an impressive .95 and the standard error is a low .39. Finally, with the Durbin-Watson statistic very near 2.00 we can be confident that first-order autocorrelation is not a problem.

Table 2.

The Civil Rights Act and Black-White
Unemployment Differences: A Three Slope Model.

Variables	Coefficient	t-statistic
Economic Control	.58	6.21
War Control	.75	2.26
1948-1964 Slope	.11	3.47
1965 Interruption	-.23	-.38
1965-1976 Slope	-.20	-3.54
1977 Interruption	.44	.81
1977-1983 Slope	.62	5.27
Constant	.12	

$R^2 = .95$ Standard Error = .39   Durbin-Watson = 1.89

DISCUSSION

What happened during the 1977-1983 period to reverse over a decade-long trend toward unemployment equality between blacks and whites? An answer to this question is elusive. To begin, a couple of possible explanations can be largely ruled out. For one, partisan control of government does not appear to hold the answer. The black-white unemployment difference lessened during the Nixon and Ford administrations, despite cuts to the Equal Employment Opportunity Commission's enforcement funds. Furthermore, the disastrous 1977-1983 years correspond closely to the Carter administration, an administration strongly committed to civil rights. To be sure, Reagan has dismantled a number of public programs beneficial to blacks over the last couple of years. However, a separate analysis indicated that the black-white unemployment difference has not increased significantly faster under Reagan.[5] Instead, the evidence suggests that the widening in the difference has progressed at a steady pace since 1977.

Changes in social attitudes also show little promise in accounting for the 1977-1983 trend. Much of the effectiveness of the 1964 Act has always depended on voluntary compliance by employers. If societal attitudes, especially those of employers, had recently become more discriminatory, perhaps voluntary compliance with the Act would have decreased. However, recent public opinion polls show no significant increase in anti-black attitudes.

Appendix A.

Black and White Unemployment Rates: 1948-1983.

	Black Rate	White Rate		Black Rate	White Rate		Black Rate	White Rate
1948	5.9	3.5	1960	10.2	4.9	1972	10.0	5.0
1949	8.9	5.6	1961	12.4	6.0	1973	8.9	4.3
1950	9.0	4.9	1962	10.9	4.9	1974	9.9	5.0
1951	5.3	3.1	1963	10.8	5.0	1975	13.9	7.8
1952	5.4	2.8	1964	9.6	4.6	1976	13.1	7.0
1953	4.5	2.7	1965	8.1	4.1	1977	13.1	6.2
1954	9.9	5.0	1966	7.3	3.3	1978	11.9	5.2
1955	8.7	3.9	1967	7.4	3.4	1979	11.3	5.1
1956	8.3	3.6	1968	6.7	3.2	1980	14.3	6.3
1957	7.9	3.8	1969	6.4	3.1	1981	15.6	6.7
1958	12.6	6.1	1970	8.2	4.5	1982	18.9	8.6
1959	10.7	4.8	1971	9.9	5.4	1983	20.6	8.6

Source: U.S. Bureau of Labor Statistics

The economy, at least, offers some clues as to what might have caused the deteriorating unemployment position for blacks during 1977-1983. First, the labor market has shifted toward high technology jobs, led by the rapid increase in the use of computers. This has been particularly true since the mid-1970s. Blacks are generally not qualified for these new jobs because they lack the necessary education and training. Second, unemployment in the traditionally black labor markets has remained high or has risen since the mid-1970s. For example, unemployment in industries with a high percentage of black workers has generally risen (e.g., the automotive industry and the textile industry). Also, unemployment among southern black farm workers has increased since the mid-1970s (Economist, 1982). Third, public sector hiring has increased slowly since the mid-1970s, and as Brown and Erie (1981) report, black equality gains from 1965 to 1976 were due greatly to increased minority hiring by government. Taken together, these three economic trends may aid in accounting for the deteriorating black unemployment position. Firm answers, however, will have to await further empirical testing.

In sum, the Civil Rights Act of 1964, perhaps more than any other piece of social legislation to emerge from the Great Society, held all the keys to ensure success. The language of Title VII unmistakably prohibits employment discrimination in hiring, firing, and compensation terms due to race. In addition, President Johnson and Congress, spurred in part by massive public support, quickly put in place additional legislation to aid in the Act's enforcement. The courts also fully and quickly obliged, deciding numerous cases in favor of the Act. Yet this study indicates convincingly that intensive government action does not always achieve its goals. Nearly 20 years after the Civil Rights Act black unemployment is still much higher than white unemployment. Even with the economy and war controlled, equalization has not been forthcoming. What is worse, after gains for blacks relative to whites during the 1965-1976 period, the following five years, 1977-1983, saw a return to increasing unemployment inequalities between blacks and whites.

NOTES

[1]For instance, the series P-60 No. 114 edition of the Current Population Reports includes as income "public assistance or welfare payments" and "Social Security" (p. 260).

[2]The U.S. Bureau of the Census, in Money Income in 1972 of Families and Persons in the United States, series P-60 No. 90, reported blacks to receive approximately six times as much of their income from welfare than whites.

[3]See: Miller v. International Paper Co., 408 f 2d 283 5th cir. 1969; Culpepper v. Reynolds Metals, 421 f 2d 888 5th cir. 1970; Cox v. United States Gypsum Co., 409 f 2d 289 7th cir. 1969; and McDonnell Douglas v. Green, 411 U.S. 792 5 fep cases 965 (1973).

[4]The war years were considered 1951-1953 and 1965-1972.

[5]An additional interruption (1982) and slope (1981-1983) were added to tap the black-white unemployment difference trend for the Reagan years. Neither the interruption or the slope were significant.

REFERENCES

Becker, Gary S. 1967. The Economics of Discrimination. Chicago: University of Chicago Press.

Bell, D. 1972. "Occupational Discrimination as a Source of Income Differences: Lessons of the 1960s." The American Economic Review 62: 363-72.

Brown, Michael K. and Steven P. Erie. 1981. "Blacks and the Legacy of the Great Society." Public Policy 29: 299-330.

Campbell, Donald T. and Thomas D. Cook. 1978. The Design and Analysis of Quasi-Experiments for Field Settings. Chicago: Rand McNally.

Darity, W. A., Jr. 1982. "Human Capita Approach to Black-White Earnings Inequality: Some Unsettled Questions." Journal of Human Resources 17: 72-93.

Economist. 1982. "Several Steps Back." 282: March 6: 21.

Farley, R. and A. Hermalin. 1972. "The 1960s: A Decade of Progress for Blacks?" Demography 9: 353-370.

Freeman, Richard B. 1973. "Decline of Labor Market Discrimination and Economic Analysis." The American Economic Review 63: 280-286.

-----. 1978. "Black Economic Gains Since the 1960s." Public Interest 50: 52-68.

Gilman, Harry. 1963. "The White/Non-White Unemployment Differential." In Human Resources in the Urban Economy, Mark Perlman, ed. Washington, D.C.: Resources for the Future, Inc. 75-113.

Gilroy, Curtis L. 1975. "Black and White Unemployment: The Dynamics of the Differential." Monthly Labor Review. Washington, D.C.: U.S. Department of Labor. 45-56.

Glenn, Norval D. 1969. "Changes in the Social and Economic Conditions of Black Americans During the 1960s." In Blacks in the United States, Norval D. Glenn and Charles M. Bonjean, ed. San Francisco: Chandler.

McCrone, Donald J. and Richard J. Hardy. 1978. "Civil Rights Policies and the Achievement of Racial Economic Equality, 1948-1975." American Journal of Political Science 22: 1-17.

Master, Stanley H. 1975. Black-White Income Differentials: Empirical Studies and Policy Simplification. New York: Academic.

Pindyck, Robert S. and Daniel L. Rubinfeld. 1981. Econometric Models and Economic Forecasts. New York: McGraw-Hill.

Smith, Ralph C. and Charles C. Holt. 1970. "A Job Search-Turnover Analysis of the Black-White Unemployment Ratio." In Industrial Relations Research Association, Proceedings of the Twenty-Third Annual Winter Meeting. 76-86.

Thurow, Lester. 1969. Poverty and Discrimination. Washington, D.C.: The Brookings Institute.

Villemez, Wayne J. and Candace Hinson Wiswell. 1978. "The Impact of Diminishing Discrimination on the Internal Size Distribution of Black Incomes: 1954-74." Social Forces 56: 1019-1034.

William P. Bridges
Wayne J. Villemez

Overeducated Minority Workers:
Does EEOC Coverage Make a Difference?

INTRODUCTION

Most research on the effects of equal employment opportunity legislation has evaluated its impact by looking at changing differentials in income or employment levels (Burstein, 1979; Freeman, 1981; Smith and Welch, 1977). These studies are essential and have the obvious advantage of considering outcome variables which are of immediate popular interest.[1] However, relative wages are only one indicator of economic opportunity and, unless one subscribes to the simplistic belief that wages correspond directly to productivity, offer an index which is contaminated by all sorts of other factors. For example, relative black incomes could have been raised only by a disproportionate influx of black workers into those occupations and industries where workers enjoy the most monopolistic and protected positions.

Although it is difficult to argue with the proposition of "fair for one, fair for all," broadening the focus beyond income or wages offers the possibility of uncovering changes at the level of job quality as well as at the level of job rewards. One would hope that the implementation of equal opportunity means extending minorities an equal chance to contribute to economic welfare as well as an equal chance to exploit market imperfections.

This chapter considers evidence on one issue within the broader topic of equity in job assignment: the relationship between federal EEO coverage and the educational over (or under) qualification of minority group workers. EEOC coverage should have effects in this domain because the basic legal initiatives which empower affirmative action remedies, Title VII of the 1964 Civil Rights Act, as amended, and Executive

72

Order 11246, prohibit discrimination both in the fact of employment (hiring, dismissal, etc.) and in the nature of employment (promotion, working conditions, etc.). This message has been clearly received by the constituency of these measures. In 1975, 51% of the actionable issues of racial discrimination reported in charges to the EEOC involved job quality issues.[2] Although the percentage was somewhat lower in 1981, 33%, job quality issues continue to loom large (EEOC, 1976:57; 1982:141).

Because education represents an investment of considerable time and foregone earnings to individuals, it is not surprising that the issue of equity in job assignment among those with equal educational attainments should be emotionally charged. Thus, it makes a considerable difference whether government efforts in promoting equality of employment opportunity coexist with a situation in which black workers, relative to whites, have too much education for their jobs, just the right amount, or not enough. Frequently, opposition to affirmative action is phrased in terms of the allegation that minorities are being hired into jobs for which they are underqualified. Although this belief may be so strongly rooted in some circles that it is no longer susceptible to empirical argument, less dogmatic audiences need more objective information about the relationship among minority group status, earned education, and education used on the job.

A related issue is posed by the question of minority underrepresentation in jobs which require high levels of formal education. For some observers, even if it can be shown that among workers with the same education, minority workers have jobs of equal standing, i.e., requiring the same level of formal education, the issue of discrimination will not have been put to rest. That is, unless the educational requirements are clearly justified by the kinds of performances entailed in these jobs, the de facto exclusion of minorities with lesser quantities of education unfairly restricts them from competing for jobs for which they are substantively qualified.[3]

While this sort of discrimination would be absent in a perfect society, it is not obvious that simple remedies would have only the intended consequences. For example, in the case of blacks, the belief that they would quickly benefit from the elimination of specious educational requirements, depends first on the assumption that there is a fixed amount of discrimination within educational levels in the hiring process. That is, if the pool of jobs not requiring a high school degree were suddenly expanded, there is no guarantee that a proportionate share of the increased number of low level jobs would be allocated to minority workers. Furthermore, such a proposal would do nothing to increase the proportion of minority workers in upper level jobs, and in all likelihood would decrease that proportion. Second, this sort of proposal assumes that a decrease in the average level of education required for jobs would be accompanied by a concomitant contraction in the proportion of workers supplying this level of education in the labor market. For any reasonable definition of the social and economic short-run, this possibility seems slight. Do those with some college education drop out of the labor market when a job which used to require some college training (police officer, perhaps) lowers that requirement, or do they force their way downward and compete for jobs which require less education than they have? This sort of problem is not dealt with adequately by the simple prescription that educational screening requirements for jobs should not exceed their education performance requirements.

Therefore, the focus here is on the broader question of whether and how minorities are able to attain jobs that make full use of their existing educational achievements. In answering this question, we shall have to confront squarely the very problem which is side-stepped by the inflated-education requirement argument, the degree to which educational requirements are administered fairly across population groups. That is, it is possible that minorities might benefit more from greater consistency in the administration of education screening criteria, than they would from the outright abolition of such requirements. Finally, although the issues go beyond the scope of this paper, inconsistency in the use of educational requirements would be predicted by one version of the "statistical discrimination" model.[4]

In the remaining sections of this chapter, we will proceed as follows: First, we shall describe two data sources on this question which are separated by almost ten years of equal employment enforcement activity. Turning to these data, we will assess patterns of over-time change in the distribution of educational over-qualification and attempt to determine how those patterns can be interpreted in terms of both statistical discrimination theory and the possibility of an EEOC enforcement impact.

DATA

Two surveys of employed persons are used to evaluate the extent of educational overqualification. The first is the well-known 1972 Quality of Employment Survey, hereafter the QES (Institute for Social Research, 1975). This was administered to a nationally representative sample of both wage and salary and self-employed workers; however, only the former are analyzed here. The second data source is a recently completed intensive survey of the population employed in the Chicago metropolitan labor market (hereafter, the Metropolitan Employer-Worker

Survey or MEWS). In this study interviews were conducted with 2712 wage and salary workers and additional interviews were completed with 1926 of the employers of these persons. Both of these samples contain highly similar measures of key variables.

In both studies workers were asked about the amount of education which their jobs required. In the QES the question was worded, "What level of formal education do you feel is needed by a person in your job?" Respondents were allowed to answer in terms of eight levels ranging from "none" to "graduate or professional school." The MEWS study was slightly different with respondents replying to two separate questions: (1) "What minimum levels of formal education is required for a person to be hired for a job like yours?" and (2) "Does the job require that much formal education or could the job be done with less formal education?" ("More" was also an acceptable response.) In order to maximize the similarity of the two surveys the MEWS responses to the first question were adjusted according to the answers to the second question. Where interviewees said the job could be done with less education, the required education level was decremented by one step; where they said more was needed an extra step was added.[5]

Levels of completed formal education were measured in terms of the same groups of educational steps and comparative distributions are also shown in Table 1. In both the required and completed educational distributions the MEWS data show a flatter distribution; not surprisingly these data also show a higher overall level of completed education which reflects, in part, the higher levels of education achieved during the 1970's. Comparative figures are also shown for the age and racial compositions of the two samples and the breakdown of each into government and private employment categories. Again the distributions are neither very comparable nor can the differences be easily reconciled.

Alternatively, the wage for each job might have been used as the dependent variable. There are, however, two advantages to the educational requirement scores used here. First, inter-racial comparisons of wage rates are necessarily muddied by the existence of numerous imperfections in the labor market, such as labor unions and professional monopolies. In examining the effects of government policy on employers, it is helpful to avoid contaminating the results with patterns which result from the actions of others factors such as schools and labor organizations. Second, the identical metric of education step obtained and education step used on the job makes the regression coefficients intuitively appealing. A slope of "1" reveals a direct trade-off of education into job complexity.

TABLE 1

Comparative distributions of required education, acquired
education, race, age, and employer type in 1972 Quality of
Employment Survey and 1981 Metropolitan Employer-Worker Survey

Educational Level Required For Job Performance	1972 QUES	1981 MEWS
Less than Grade School*	0.0%	0.9%
Grades 1-8	12.2%	2.3%
Some High School	11.0%	22.2%
High School Completion	45.0%	30.8%
Some College	15.9%	21.5%
College Completion	9.3%	16.4%
Graduate or Professional School	6.6%	5.9%
Total	100.0%	100.0%
	(843.)**	(2003.)

Education level completed		
None	0.0%	0.1%
Grades 1-8	8.7%	1.0%
Some High School	11.7%	3.7%
High School Completion	39.2%	29.9%
Some College	23.9%	27.6%
College Completion	8.5%	19.8%
Graduate or Professional School	7.9%	17.8%
Total	100.0%	100.0%
	(843.)	(2003.)

Race		
White, Other	90.3%	85.0%
Black	9.7%	14.4%
Total	100.0%	100.0%
	(843.)	(2003.)

Type of Employer		
Private	83.0%	83.7%
Public	17.0%	16.3%
Total	100.0%	100.0%
	(843.)	(2003.)

Age		
Mean (Years)	37.2	37.7

* Respondents in both surveys who said "None" or "No set level"; were excluded. The
small number in the MEWS study who appear in this category were those who said
they needed some grade school to be hired but who said the job could be done with
less education.

** Metropolitan Sample only. Frequencies are weighted by sampling weights provided by
ISR.

OPERATIONALIZATION

The primary mode of analysis in this chapter will be a series of regression equations with the amount of education required for job performance used as the dependent variable. The most basic models employed are those shown below (there is one model for each level of i):

$$Y_i = b_{1i} X_{1i} + b_{2i} X_{2i} + b_{3i} X_{3i} + e_i$$

Where: Y_i=Education step required in survey i

X_{1i}=Education step completed in survey i

X_{2i}=Race in survey i

X_{3i}=Age in years in survey i

e_i=Error in survey i

i=1 for 1972 Quality of Employment Survey

=2 for 1981 Metropolitan Employer-Worker Survey

To each of these basic models additional terms are added to test various hypotheses. The premise underlying this procedure is that the effect of race on required education net of years of education actually obtained indicates the extent of under- or overqualification present for black workers relative to whites. A negative sign on this term indicates job over-qualification for blacks relative to whites. Although our primary interest in this paper is directed at racial under- or overqualification, we briefly consider the levels of qualification held by members of the two sexes.

FINDINGS

In Table 2 several regression models are presented for the 1972 Quality of Employment Survey. Column 1 presents the model which provides the best overall fit to the data and Columns 2 and 3 provide specific tests of some alternative hypothesis. There are several important results evident in this table. The relationship between acquired and required education is strongly positive, and more significantly less than 1.00. Accompanying this relationship is a coefficient for the black worker variable which is significantly negative, indicating that in general blacks were educationally overqualified for the jobs in which they were employed relative to whites. For example, at age 25, white workers in the private sector with education completed through step "6" (4 years of college) are employed in jobs with an average required educational step level of 5.25; similarly qualified black workers would be found in jobs with a step value of 4.89, slightly less than some college education. While it is not apparent from the basic equation, both the

TABLE 2

Regression Coefficients of Education Step Needed on Current
Job Data from 1972 Quality of Employment Survey

Independent Variable	Model 1	Model 2	Model 3
Intercept	.680	.693	7.67
	(.148)	(.150)	(.150)
Education step completed	.725	.	.727
	(.025)		(.025)
Race (Black=1)	-.362	-.571	-.386
	(.101)	(.356)	(.102)
Age (years)	.009	.009	.009
	(.002)	(.002)	(.002)
Government employee	.342	.342	.325
	(.0834)	(.084)	(.084)
Education if black	.	.774	.
		(.086)	
Education if white	.	.721	.
		(.023)	
Small establishment	.	.	-.044
			(.059)
Sex (Male=1)	.	.	-1.39
			(.061)
R-squared (adj.)	.5655	.5652	.5674
Number of cases	843	843	843

"average" black and white workers, i.e., those at the mean on
all independent variables would be assigned to the jobs below
their levels of acquired education. Thus, the overqualification
of blacks is true in both a relative and an absolute sense.

Column 2 of this table evaluates a model in which the
education coefficients for blacks and whites are allowed to vary
independently. The difference in slopes is not statistically
significant, and even if it were, the black slope is greater than
the white one. While we will reevaluate this result in other
contexts, it appears that the degree of overqualification is
relatively constant across the educational spectrum.[6] Column 3
modifies the basic model by including terms for those working in
small establishments (with fewer than 100 employees and for
gender). While the former is not significant, the latter indicates
a tendency for males to be in jobs where they are overqualified
relative to females. This finding raises the possibility that a
parallel analysis for sex differences might be conducted
alongside the one for race differences. We have not pursued this
course because the absolute size of the sex difference is small,
because it disappears in subsequent equations, and because the

direction is inconsistent with the underlying gist of this analysis. (Remember that at most levels of education all workers are overqualifed for their jobs.)

Applying these same three models to the 1981 MEWS survey data produces the results displayed in Table 3. On the whole, the coefficients are extraordinarily similar to those in Table 2, a refreshing occurrence in an area where statistical outcomes are notoriously ephemeral. The effect of age is identical in the two studies and the coefficient for acquired education is the same to two-digit accuracy. In light of this near perfect replication for two variables, we note that the effect of race, while still negative and still statistically significant, is smaller than in the 1972 data. (The reduction fails to meet conventional criteria for statistical significance, e.g., the hypothesis that the 1981 value is equal to or smaller than -.362 has a p value of .1 on a one-tailed t-test.)

There are other similarities in the results for the two surveys. For example, Table 3 yields the same conclusion as Table 2 with regard to different education slopes for black and white workers. Furthermore, jobs with government employers continue to require a statistically significant greater amount of education than private industry jobs. On the change side, the small gender difference in the 1972 table has disappeared completely, while the negative effect of working for a small employer has become more important.

Returning to the decreased race effect in 1981, it is interesting to consider whether the result might be associated with an equal opportunity enforcement impact. Thus, in subsequent tables, this race effect will be compared across years in different categories of employers. Specifically, we shall make direct comparisons among those who work for the government, for large private employers (i.e., those with at least 100 employees) and for small private employers. Subsequently, we shall make some indirect assessments for whether the differences between the two surveys can be attributed to other factors besides the passage of time, possibly EEO effect accompanying the passage of time.

Because federal Civil Rights legislation affords differential coverage to business depending upon their size, it is relevant to ask whether differences in educational discrimination can be found which correspond to these coverages. For most employees except those of the federal government, the Civil Rights Act of 1964 established exclusions for employers below a certain size limit. In 1965, this limit was to have been 100 employees, and it was to have been reduced by 25 employees for each of the next three years. In the Civil Rights Act of 1972, the exclusion was again legislated downward to its present level of 15 employees (which became effective in 1974; see U.S.

TABLE 3

Regression Coefficients of Education Step
Needed on Current Job Data from 1981 Metropolitan
Employer-Worker Survey

Independent Variable	Model 1	Model 2	Model 3
Intercept	.347	.335	4.05
	(.114)	(.118)	(.118)
Education step completed	.730**	.	.727
	(.017)	.	(.017)
Race (Black=1)	-.284**	-.183	-.290**
	(.059)	(.249)	(.059)
Age (years)	.009**	.009**	.008**
	(.002)	(.002)	(.002)
Government employee	.127*	.127*	.132*
	(.057)	(.057)	(.057)
Education if black	.	.712**	.
		(.046)	
Education if white	.	.733**	.
		(.018)	
Small establishment	.	.	-.116**
			(.042)
Sex (Male=1)	.	.	.024
			(.041)
R-squared (adj.)	.4897	.4985	.5003
Number of cases	1994	1994	1994

---

*t significant p .05
**t significant p .01
Standard errors in parenthesis

House of Representatives, Sub-Committee on the Judiciary,
1971; 1981). Furthermore, administrative regulations of the
EEOC require employers of 100 or more individuals to file
annual EEO-1 reports which detail race and sex breakdowns of
each employer's labor force in major occupational categories.
For Federal Government employees explicit protections of equal
employment opportunity are established in Section 717 of Title
VII and the Civil Service Reform Act of 1967.
    As a first approximation to uncovering the effects of such
differences, we have split both the 1972 and 1981 samples into
three subgroups for further analysis: (1) employees of
governmental units (including federal, state, and local); (2)
employees of large private establishments (again using the 100
cutoff); and (3) employees of small private establishments.
Table 4 contains regression results for these subgroups as well

TABLE 4

Regression Coefficients of Education Step Needed on Current Job
Separate Models for Government, Large Private
and Small Private Employers. 1972 and 1981 Survey Data

Independent Variable	Total Sample	Public	Large Private	Small Private
A. 1972 Quality of Employment Survey Metropolitan Sample				
Intercept	.735	.224	.666	1.050
	(.155)	(.346)	(.260)	(.220)
Education step completed	.722**	.853**	.750**	.620**
	(.025)	(.046)	(.042)	(.040)
Race (Black=1)	-.367**	-.056	-.333*	-.620**
	(.101)	(.182)	(.166)	(.173)
Age (years)	.009**	.011*	.007	.010**
	(.002)	(.005)	(.004)	(.003)
Government employee	.304**	.	.	.
	(.089)	.	.	.
Small private empl.	-.077	.	.	.
	(.065)			
R-squared (adj.)	.5655	.7276	.4937	.4400
Number of cases	843	143	343	357
B. 1981 Metropolitan Employer-Worker Survey				
Intercept	.443	-.039	.596	.362
	(.117)	(.267)	(.164)	(.201)
Education step completed	.728**	.886**	.695**	.694**
	(.017)	(.037)	(.024)	(.032)
Race (Black=1)	-.300**	-.187	-.414**	-.136
	(.058)	(.105)	(.083)	(.122)
Age (years)	.088**	-.001	.009**	.010**
	(.002)	(.004)	(.002)	(.002)
Government employee	.075	.	.	.
	(.058)			
Small private empl.	-.163**	.	.	.
	(.045)			
R-squared (adj.)	.5036	.6518	.4647	.4323
Number of cases	2003	322	1031	638

----

*t significant p .05
**t significant p .01
Standard errors in parenthesis

as a matching model for the overall samples which can be used to test statistically the contribution of different regression parameters across subgroups. This aggregate model differs slightly from those we have previously examined insofar as it contains dummy variables for both government employment and for small private employment. Furthermore in the case of the MEWS data, there is a slightly larger case base due to the inclusion of those government employees for whom an establishment size was not reported (these no longer need be regarded as missing).

Beginning with panel A, which details the outcome for the 1972 QES sample, a fairly clear-cut pattern unfolds. Black overqualification, as we might have expected, is practically non-existent in the context of government employment, is at a moderate level in the large private employment sector, and appears to be particularly virulent in the small private employer subgroup. This seems quite consistent with the notion that intensity of coverage under fair employment legislation does make a difference. However, another possibility comes to light when changes in the coefficient for acquired education are examined across these same subgroups. Quite simply, as the slope of required education on acquired education becomes steeper, the black-white difference shrinks noticeably. Perhaps, therefore, the pattern of results in this part of the table could be easily explained without invoking any enforcement effect at all. A simple explanation for the steeper slopes in government and large private establishments might be that formal education enhances job performance more directly in bureaucratic work settings that depend on exercise of technical expertise acquired through formal training. (For a related argument in the education-income relationship see Stolzenberg, 1978.)

With these alternatives in mind, the results in panel B become especially meaningful. Once again, the government sector is distinguished by a very strong relationship between acquired and required education and by a low discrimination effect (which is greater than the comparable effect in 1972, however). But in the private sector there is a dramatic turnabout. The phenomenon of black overqualification virtually disappears in the small establishment context, but increases in the large private sector. This result seems to fit poorly with the EEOC enforcement interpretation, since we might have expected some reduction of discrimination in both the large and small private sectors - especially in the latter where coverage was being systematically extended downward - thus the increase in the large establishment subgroups coefficient is puzzling. What can account for these divergences?

Several possibilities exist. The first is that the relationship between race and required education may not be

FIGURE 1

EFFECT OF RACE ON EDUCATION STEP REQUIRED
VARYING MAXIMUM SIZES OF ESTABLISHMENT
COMPARISON OF 1972 QES AND 1981 MEWS

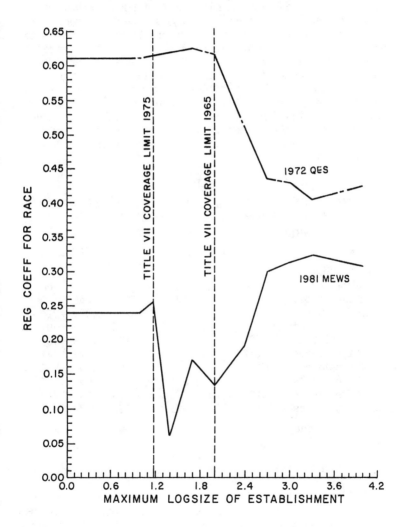

uniform in the below 100 establishment size category. The EEOC enforcement explanation would gain credibility were there seem to be striking differences in the covered and uncovered portions of the small establishment portions of the sample.   Another explanation is that the differences between the 1972 and 1981 samples are not attributable to temporal change at all, but instead reflect the importance of city size, geography, or some other variable. To further explore these possibilities some supplementary analyses were conducted.

One manipulation that is particularly informative is to inspect the change in the regression coefficient for race as observations from larger and larger establishment size categories are added to the analysis. While this technique does not allow one to make direct comparisons between regression results for larger and smaller establishments directly, it is well suited to investigating the change in slope which accompanies change in establishment size. In Table 5, the results of this analysis are presented in numerical form and Figure 1 provides a graphic summary.

TABLE 5

Effect of Race on Education Level Required for Job
Unstandardized Regression Coefficients in Progressively
Larger Maximum Establishment Sizes

Maximum Size of Establishment	1972 QES			1981 MEWS		
	B	se	N	B	se	N
9 Employees	-.611	.250	124	-.240	.256	142
14 Employees				-.255	.221	210
24 Employees				-.062	.183	307
49 Employees	-.626	.188	286	-.171	.146	465
99 Employees	-.617	.173	357	-.136	.122	642
249 Employees				-.192	.100	882
499 Employees	-.435	.133	511	-.301	.093	1086
999 Employees	-.429	.129	566	-.315	.084	1273
1999 Employees	-.405	.126	603	-.325	.079	1413
None	-.425	.119	700	-.308	.069	1677

For the 1972 data, this technique confirms what we already knew - establishments below size 100 provide a particularly fertile climate for the growth of black overqualification. In the 1981 data, however, a different story emerges. When the size 15 threshold is crossed, the minimum establishment size covered by Title VII since 1974, the effect of race diminishes noticeably.   Thus, the lowest associations between race and overqualification would be found in establishments employing between 15 and 100 people. However, beyond that point there is a marked increase in the level of black overqualification.

Before drawing conclusions from this analysis, it will be useful to consider some alternative hypotheses that might explain the drastic differences in result for employees of small private establishments in the two surveys. One possibility is that the difference for this subgroup, and only this subgroup, is attributable to some difference between the Chicago SMSA and other metropolitan areas. To examine this possibility, the QES data were rerun with the sample split between the 12 largest metropolitan areas and other metro locations. The coefficients for race were as follows: For larger private establishments the small city coefficient is - .31 and the big city coefficient is -.41; for small private establishments the small city coefficient is -.79 and the big city coefficient is -.42. Thus the extremely large negative value for small private employers in the QES data is partly colored by the inclusion of cases from metropolitan areas which are not very comparable to the 1981 study areas. However, the effect remains sizeable even in the big city group and it is doubtful that city size alone explains why the 1981 race coefficient is as small as it is in the "under-100" private sector subgroup.

A further indirect test of temporal change vs. geographic difference can be carried out by looking at differences between MEWS respondents who have been in their present jobs for shorter and longer periods of time. If the effects are due to temporal change, presumably there should be less overqualification among more recent additions to the firm's labor force. Of course, this test by itself is not conclusive but the results do offer an opportunity for disconfirming an enforcement effect. In the small private subgroup the race coefficient is -.063 for those with fewer than five years of tenure and -.181 for those with five years or more of tenure. (It should be added that neither coefficient is statistically different from zero.)

Before discussing these results, we want to address one other topic with empirical data, the issue of job underqualification. The fact that both blacks and whites are on the average educationally overqualified for their current positions, does not preclude the possibility that some members of both race groups have too little education for their current positions. However, to investigate this phenomenon requires a different analytic approach than the one we have followed so far. In Table 6, we have presented the results occurring when a newly constructed variable, job underqualification is cross-classified by race and survey. This variable is simply the algebraic difference between each respondent's level of acquired education and his or her level of required education dichotomized between negative and all other scores. What is readily apparent in both surveys is that whites have a greater tendency to be underqualified for their jobs than blacks do. While there are too few cases to allow for separate comparisons in the subgroups examined above, the lowering of the black - white gap in this measure again is consistent with a positive EEO enforcement effect.

TABLE 6

Extent of Job Underqualification by Race.
1972 Quality of Employment Survey and
1981 Metropolitan Employer-Worker Survey.

Race	Percent Underqualified for Current Job	
	1972 QUE	1981 MEWS
Black	9.7%	4.5%
	(82.)	(288.)
White	16.8%	6.3%
	(761.)	(1715.)

CONCLUSIONS

To summarize, we cannot rule out the existence of an EEO coverage effect on discrimination in job assignment. The size threshold of 15 workers appears to be related to change in the size of the overqualification effect, and this pattern only appears in the survey data collected after that size limit took effect.   Further, there are consistent differences between employees of government units and others in the extent of overqualification.   Finally, more recently hired employees appear to suffer less of this form of discrimination than others. What remains to be considered is why the gains of the nine-year period should be restricted to the small private sector. Here we wish to suggest two possibilities which are not mutually exclusive. The first is that enforcement of controversial policy initiatives is subject to rebound effects.   As a group comes under the protective coverage of "fairness" legislation, the initial response is one of improved opportunity. As time passes, however, previously established ways of doing business reassert themselves and some of the earlier gains are lost.

The second piece of the explanation may have to do with the concept of statistical discrimination mentioned earlier. The data we have been examining are quite consistent with the formal model of statistical   discrimination developed by Aigner and Cain which they call the "different means" model. Accepting momentarily the idea of a rebound effect, the question is what explains the kind of practices that employers bounce back toward. One possibility is that they revert most readily to policies which have some utility and are based to some degree on "rational" ways of doing business. And, the major underpinning of the statistical discrimination is the idea that group discrimination is rational when other performance indicators provide imperfect information.

At this point, this should be regarded only as a hypothesis meriting further investigation. There are, in fact, many reasons to be skeptical of this possibility. One is that the "rebound" can be easily explained by other mechanisms such as the informal opposition of majority group workers. That is, one of the ways in which the level of black and white relative job qualifications can become equalized is for the level of white absolute overqualification to increase. Were this the case, white opposition might be expected and might be expected to be more or less effective depending on other characteristics of the firm's environment. A second for caution is that with the pressure on for equal treatment of minority and majority workers, employers might be expected to seek other selection and evaluation devices which obviate their need to reply on group properties in the hiring decision. Again both of these issues are empirical, but are outside the scope of the present inquiry.

FOOTNOTES

[1]With regard to wages, Christopher Jencks, after surveying much of the literature, concludes, "In light of all of this, I do not see how (Thomas) Sowell or other free market economists can deny that Title VII increased black workers' earnings." (1983:13).

[2]We consider job quality issues those which were classified by the EEOC as involving wages, promotion, demotion, seniority, job classification, and terms and conditions of employment. Employment access issues (hiring, discharge, layoff, and recall) contributed 34%. The total number of issues in race related charges was 68,487.

[3]The existence of education requirements unrelated to subsequent job performance is a central tenet of labor market theories subscribing to the "screening hypothesis." According to its proponents, education is used to sort and classify job applicants even when it is not directly related to on-the-job productivity (See Arrow, 1973; Wolphin, 1977. For an ingenious apology for such arrangements, see Spence, 1973).

[4]The essence of this model is that when certain achieved factors such as education are used as screening devices, individual minority group members experience invidious treatment because of "information" problems confronted by employers during the hiring process. For a more complete treatment see Aigner and Cain, 1977; for an application, Blau and Kahn, 1981.

[5]One further complication is that the MEWS combined those who said "No set level" with the group saying "None" and it also combined the QES categories of "Some grade school." The former were dropped from the analysis and the latter two were aggregated in the QES to attain comparability.

Because the measures of educational requirements are based on respondents' self-reports, the following analysis might be biased if black respondents over- or underestimated the credentials needed for their jobs relative to whites' estimates. In the MEWS study, there is information available which suggests this is not a serious problem. For about two-thirds of the jobs in this sample, information was gathered from employers about their own practices with regard to educational requirements. These data reveal the same pattern as the respondent-generated data - jobs held by blacks require less education on the average than jobs held by whites.

[6]Note that the model used to test for black-white interaction is one which forces the slopes for all other variables to be equal. While there is no a priori theoretical rationale for expecting other slopes to be different, allowing them to vary might alter the results shown in column 2. When such a model is estimated for the QES data, there is no change in the conclusion just presented; the slope for whites is .725 and for blacks is .723.

[7]Once again this conclusion comes from a model in which slopes for other independent variables have been restricted to be equal for blacks and whites. When all coefficients are free to vary across race, the white education coefficient is larger than the black by a greater amount than in Table 3 (.735 vs. .681). The difference however is not statistically significant, $t=1.067$, $p=.28$.

REFERENCES

Aigner, Dennis and Glen Cain. 1977. "Statistical Theories of Discrimination in Labor Markets." Industrial and Labor Relations Review. 30 (Jan): 175-87.

Arrow, Kenneth. 1973. "Higher Education as a Filter." Journal of Public Economics. 2 (July) 193-216.

Blau, Francine and Lawrence Kahn. 1981. "Race and Sex Differences in Quits by Young Workers." Industrial and Labor Relations Review. 34 (July): 563-577.

Burstein, Paul. 1979. "Equal Employment Opportunity Legislation and the Income of Women and Nonwhites." American Sociological Review. 44 (June): 367-91.

Freeman, Richard. 1981. "Black Economic Progress after 1964; Who Has Gained and Why." Studies in Labor Markets. (ed.) (Chicago: University of Chicago Press).

Institute for Social Research. 1975. The 1972-73 Quality of Employment Survey. (Institute for Social Research: Ann Arbor).

Jencks, Christopher, 1983. "Special Treatment for Blacks?" New York Review of Books (March 10): 13-19.

Smith, James and Finis Welch. 1977. "Black-White Male Wage Ratios: 1960-70." American Economic Review 67 (June): 323-338.

Spence, Michael. 1973. "Job Market Signaling." Quarterly Journal of Economics. 87 (August): 355-379.

Stolzenberg, Ross M. 1978. "Bringing the Boss Back In: Employer Size, Employee Schooling, and Labor Market Achievement." American Sociological Review. 43 (December): 813-828.

U.S. Department of Labor, Bureau of Labor Statistics. 1982. Employment and Earnings. 29 (December): 18.

U.S. Department of Labor, Bureau of Labor Statistics. 1981. Employment and Earnings. 28 (December): 101.

U.S. Equal Opportunity Commission. 1982. Sixteenth Annual Report. Washington: Government Printing Office.

U.S. Equal Opportunity Commission. 1976. Tenth Annual Report. Washington: Government Printing Office.

U.S. House of Representatives, Committee on the Judiciary, 1981. "The Civil Rights Acts of 1957, 1960, 1964, and 1968,

As Amended Through the 96th Congress" (Committee Print). (Washington: Government Printing Office)

U.S. House of Representatives, Committee on the Judiciary, 1971. "The Civil Rights Acts of 1957, 1960, 1964, and 1968." (Committee Print). (Washington: Government Printing Office)

Wolphin Kenneth. 1977. "Education and Screening." American Economic Review. 67 (December): 949-58.

Part III
The Public Sector and Affirmative Action: An Assessment

Lee Sigelman
N. Jospeh Cayer

Minorities, Women, and Public Sector Jobs:
A Status Report

Approximately fifteen million Americans work as civilian employees in some arm of federal, state, or local government. The sheer size of the public sector workforce makes implementation by government agencies a key to the success of equal employment opportunity and affirmative action programs, which aim at producing "measureable, yearly improvements in hiring, training and promotion of minorities and females" (Equal Employment Opportunity Commission, 1974s: 3). In monitoring trends in the job status of minorities and women within the public sector, then, we go far toward gauging the extent to which these groups are succeeding in their quest for individual and collective mobility.

In an earlier paper, we used data gathered by the Equal Employment Opportunity Commission (EEOC) to assess the status of minorities and women in state and local governments as of 1973 and 1975, shortly after the amendment in 1972 of Title VII of the 1964 Civil Rights Act, which extended federal prohibitions against discrimination in hiring, firing, promotion, compensation, and other conditions of employment to state and local governments (Cayer and Sigelman, 1980). We addressed two specific sets of questions. First, where did minorities and women stand with respect to both the quantity and the quality of the jobs they held in state and local government agencies? Second, to what extent could changes in the status of minorities and women be observed over the course of the 1973-1975 period?

The racial/ethnic and sexual composition of the state and local government workforce, we found, changed between 1973 and 1975, with the percentage of white males decreasing and the percentage of employees in every other racial/ethnic and sexual

91

category increasing. Nevertheless, in 1975 white males still comprised more than half of the state and local government workforce. We also discovered that minority and female employees had made little headway in terms of the quality of the positions they held, as indicated by differentials between them and white males in median salary levels. With the sole exception of Asian American males, no group's median salary came close to that of white males. This salary gap was especially pronounced for women, who received lower salaries than men in every racial/ethnic category. Further analysis indicated that minorities were relatively numerous in functional areas that make extensive use of unskilled labor and were much less in evidence in fields where professional training was important or where unions or employee organizations were strong. Women did especially well in fields dominated by jobs stereotyped as "women's work" but fared less well in other fields. White males drew the highest median salary in each functional field of state and local government, with minority males almost always ranking second, white females third, and minority females fourth.

In sum, the 1973-1975 figures indicated that minorities and women had made some measurable progress, although they had not yet overcome the historic legacy of white male domination of state and local government jobs. In terms of the quality of the jobs they held, minorities and women had made very little progress.

Our purpose is twofold. First, we update our earlier status report to include the 1975-1980 period. This will allow us to determine whether the trends we uncovered for the brief 1973-1975 period continued in the ensuing years. Second, we expand our status report by differentiating among state, county, and municipal governments. This will allow us to determine at which levels of government minorities and women do best and at which levels they do worst. For comparative purposes, we also examine the employment of minorities and women in the federal government. Unfortunately, workforce data pertaining specifically to state, county, and municipal governments rather than to the state and local sector as an aggregate are available only for 1975 and 1978, so our intergovernmental comparisons cannot be undertaken for the full 1973-1980 period. A three-year or even a seven-year interval is a short period for gauging workforce composition trends. However, during the mid-1970s the impetus for affirmative action was at its zenith, so if equal employment opportunity and affirmative action programs have had any measurable impact, that impact should show up in the workforce data for this particular period.

The Equal Employment Opportunity Act of 1972 is only one of a host of factors affecting the status of minorities and

women in the public service.   Other studies have examined
economic,   social,   and   political   factors   bearing   on   the
composition of the state and local government workforce (e.g.,
Borcher, 1982; Dye and Renick, 1981; Eisinger, 1982a, 1982b;
Hall and Saltzstein, 1977; Hutchins and Sigelman, 1981; Meier,
1978; Sigelman, 1976; Sigelman and Karnig, 1977; Welch, Karnig,
and Eribes, 1983a, 1983b).   While the 1972 act has not been the
sole motivator of change, it does provide the legal framework
that has been responsible for prodding government jurisdictions
into action.   As the enforcement agency for the act, EEOC
monitors implementation at the state and local levels, and its
reports provide the most comprehensive overview of the
employment status of minorities and women in state and local
governments.   In relying upon these data, we build not only upon
our own earlier study but also upon several other studies that
have used similar approaches and data sets (e.g., Benokraitis and
Feagin, 1978; Elling, 1983; Henderson, 1978; Kranz, 1976; Rose
and Chia, 1978; Smith, 1980).

DATA AND METHODS

Before proceeding any further, we need to describe the
data sources upon which our analysis is based.   The EEOC, as the
agency charged with monitoring the progress of state and local
government agencies toward equal employment opportunity and
affirmative action goals, conducts periodic surveys of the state
and local government workforce.   At this time, four such
surveys have been conducted, in 1973, 1975, 1978, and 1980
(EEOC, 1974b, 1977, 1980, 1982).   These "EEO-4" surveys, as
they are known, are sent to all state governments and to a
sample of local governments stratified by employment size and
type of jurisdiction; for example, all local jurisdictions with 100
or more employees are surveyed, but only 15 percent of those
with fewer than 25 employees are surveyed in a given year.   The
data from these surveys are adjusted to account for non-
responding and non-sampled jurisdictions in order to produce
valid estimates of the population of state and local government
employees.

Because these data are based on samples, they are subject
to error.   However, because they are based on very large and
carefully drawn samples, such error is a relatively minor
concern.   For example, according to the EEOC's 1980 survey
there were some 101,134 Spanish-surnamed male state and local
government employees (see Table 1 below); this estimate should
not be taken literally, but its standard error is so small that we
can be 95 percent confident that the actual number of Spanish-
surname male state and local government employees in 1980 was
between 100,000 and 102,200.   The same holds for the EEOC

median salary estimates, which, even for the smallest category of employees (American Indian females), are subject to an error of only $374 above or below the 1980 estimate of $11,404 (see Table 2 below).

Our status report focuses primarily upon data from the 1973 and 1980 surveys, the earliest and the latest that the EEOC has conducted; we also use the 1975 figures to help update the findings of our previous study, which catalogued the 1973-1975 trends. Unfortunately our comparison of the performance of the various levels of government cannot be based on the 1973 and 1980 data, which EEOC has not disaggregated according to level of government. The 1975 and 1978 EEOC reports were, however, disaggregated in this fashion, and we have accordingly employed 1975 and 1978 as our base years in making intergovernmental comparisons. In this part of our analysis, we also report on the status of minorities and women in the federal government, making use of the 1975 and 1978 reports published by the federal monitoring agency (Civil Service Commission, 1975; Office of Personnel Management, 1978). The reliability of these federal workforce data is no less impressive than that of the state and local workforce data.

THE OVERALL PICTURE, 1973-1980

The Quantitative Dimension

We noted in our earlier study that between 1973 and 1975 state and local government agencies became somewhat less dominated by white males, whose share of the workforce fell from 54.7 to 51.1 percent. Table 1, which shows the workforce composition figures for the entire 1973-1980 period, indicates that the trend toward greater employment of minorities and women continued after 1975, with the white male percentages of the state and local government workforce falling to 47.7 by 1980. Of course, any decline in the relative number of jobs held by white males could have been offset by an increase in the size of the state and local government workforce, which in fact grew by more than 88,000 employees in the 1975-1980 period alone; in a period of expansion, white males could have gotten a smaller relative share of a larger pie and ended up better off, in the aggregate, because of it. But this was most emphatically not the case, as Table 1 indicates, for the number of jobs held by white males declined not only relatively but absolutely as well. As the total number of positions in state and local governments nationwide increased by more than 88,000 from 1975 to 1980, the number of white male employees decreased by more than 90,000, continuing a trend that had been evident in the 1973-1975 data. For the 1973-1980 period, nearly 180,000 jobs at the state and local level were lost by white males while the overall

TABLE 1

Composition of State and Local Governmental Employment, 1973-1980

	1973		1975		1980	
Group	No.	%	No.	%	No.	%
White Male	2,084,225	(54.7)	1,993,154	(51.1)	1,902,512	(47.7)
White Female	1,031,060	(27.1)	1,109,119	(28.4)	1,243,213	(31.2)
Black Male	287,230	(7.5)	317,374	(8.1)	313,758	(7.9)
Black Female	236,112	(6.2)	284,369	(7.3)	304,965	(7.6)
Spanish-Surnamed Male	86,266	(2.3)	98,285	(2.5)	101,134	(2.5)
Spanish-Surnamed Female	38,331	(1.0)	49,159	(1.3)	61,449	(1.5)
Asian Male	11,671	(0.3)	13,565	(0.3)	21,848	(0.5)
Asian Female	10,096	(0.3)	12,661	(0.3)	20,705	(0.5)
Indian Male	6,803	(0.2)	6,868	(0.2)	10,799	(0.3)
Indian Female	3,347	(0.1)	4,014	(0.1)	7,048	(0.2)
Other Male	10,221	(0.3)	6,262	(0.2)	NA	
Other Female	3,146	(0.1)	4,450	(0.1)	NA	
TOTAL	3,808,538	(100.0)	3,899,280	(99.9)*	3,987,431	(99.9)*

*Varies from 100.0 percent due to rounding. Data are from EEOC, Minorities and Women in State and Local Government, 1973 (Washington, D.C.: Government Printing Office, 1974); EEOC, Minorities & Women in State and Local Government, 1975 (Washington: Government Printing Office, 1977); and EEOC, Job Patterns for Minorities & Women in State and Local Government, 1980 (Washington, D.C.: Government Printing Office, 1982).

TABLE 2

Median Salary and Advantage Index, By Group, 1973-1980

	1973		1975		1980	
Group	Salary	Index	Salary	Index	Salary	Index
White Male	9,873	(1.00)	$11,631	(1.00)	$15,627	(1.00)
White Female	7,069	(.72)	8,250	(.71)	11,559	(.74)
Black Male	7,912	(.80)	9,444	(.81)	12,380	(.79)
Black Female	6,886	(.70)	7,925	(.68)	10,792	(.69)
Spanish-Surnamed Male	7,976	(.81)	9,613	(.83)	13,628	(.87)
Spanish-Surnamed Female	6,540	(.66)	7,668	(.66)	10,865	(.70)
Asian Male	12,663	(1.28)	14,496	(1.25)	19,428	(1.25)
Asian Female	9,114	(.92)	10,353	(.89	14,265	(.91)
Indian Male	8,778	(.89)	10,482	(.90)	14,391	(.92)
Indian Female	6,679	(.68)	7,883	(.68)	11,404	(.73)
Other Male	8,976	(.91)	NA		NA	
Other Female	7,415	(.75)	NA		NA	
TOTAL	8,568	(.87)	9,827	(.84)	13,321	(.85)

Data are from the same sources as in Table 1.

number of positions at the state and local level grew by almost exactly the same number. Accordingly, the white male percentage of the state and local government workforce declined by seven full percentage points in only a seven-year span of time.

Who benefited from the declining number of jobs held by white males? Between 1973 and 1980 men and women in every other racial/ethnic category (blacks, the Spanish-surnamed, Asian Americans, and American Indians) increased the absolute number and the relative share of positions they held in state and local government. The most dramatic gains, though, were registered by white females, who occupied approximately 212,000 more positions in 1980 than they held in 1973, thereby increasing their share of the state and local government workforce from 27.1 in 1973 to 31.2 percent in 1980. Most of this increase came between 1975 and 1980, a period in which white females gained approximately 134,000 positions and increased their workforce share by 2.8 percentage points. Among the remaining groups penetration into state and local governmental jobs increased more or less on an across-the-board basis, the exception being black males, who held slightly fewer jobs in 1980 than they had in 1975. Spanish-surnamed males did somewhat better, managing to increase the number of jobs they held slightly and to maintain the same relative share of positions in 1980 as they had held in 1975. Black and Spanish-surnamed females and Asian and Indian males and females all made fairly substantial breakthroughs between 1975 and 1980 in terms of the number of positions they occupied.

By 1980, then, the state and local government workforce had become a good deal more representative, in a demographic sense, than it was in 1973, the first year after the 1972 amendment of the Civil Rights Act of 1964 extended federal anti-discrimination provisions to state and local governmental jurisdictions. The once-dominant numerical position of white males had declined markedly, and every other group had gained in the absolute number and the proportional share of state and local governmental jobs it held. The most impressive gains on the quantitative dimension were scored by women, especially white women, although in 1980 the number of jobs held by women in each racial/ethnic category was still smaller than the number held by men. So while substantial progress was made, much also remained to be done.

The Qualitative Dimension

Did minorities and women make more progress on the qualitative dimension of employment in the state and local government after 1975 than they had made between 1973 and 1975? Table 2 presents the median salary levels of men and women in each racial/ethnic category, along with a salary advantage index for each group. We calculated the advantage index by dividing the median salary for each group by the median salary for white males during the same year. Thus the advantage index for white males is always 1.00, and variations above or below the median white male salary are indicated by advantage ratios higher or lower than 1.00.

Between 1973 and 1980 the median salary of state and local government employees rose appreciably, going from $8,568 to $13,321, an increase of almost $5,000. Each group, without exception, shared in this trend, with the overall increase being roughly approximated, in a proportional sense, in the median salary increment of every racially-ethnically- and sexually-defined category of employees. So the increasing wealth (or, some would say, the progressive impoverishment) of state and local government employees was shared more or less equally.

However, there is equality and there is equality. The fact that 1973-1980 median salary increments were more or less proportional across groups means, in effect, that a situation of considerable inequality was frozen in place. That is, in 1973 white males enjoyed a sizeable salary advantage over members of every other group except Asian males, and the personnel developments of the 1970s did nothing to challenge the advantage white males enjoyed. In fact, comparison of the 1973 and 1980 advantage index scores reveals that there was essentially no movement in the standing of minorities and women relative to the standing of white males. As a consequence, it was not less true in 1980 than it had been seven years earlier that women were at a considerable salary disadvantage to men in the same racial/ethnic category and that black, Spanish-surnamed, and Indian males were at a considerable salary disadvantage to white males. Between 1973 and 1980, then, little or no progress was made toward offsetting the disadvantage of minorities and women on the qualitative dimension of employment in state and local government.

The Newly Hired

It is unrealistic to expect large-scale changes in the status of minorities and women to occur in only a few years. Even if there were very widespread commitment to equal opportunity and affirmative action and there were qualified minority and female applicants for every open position in state and local government, it would be mathematically impossible for there to be extremely rapid progress toward equal opportunity and affirmative action goals. As employees leave government service and as new positions are created, openings are generated -- openings that are targets of opportunity for minorities and women. But the state and local government workforce is very large and the number of job openings at any point in time is relatively small. This means that change, if and when it comes, will be rather sluggish, for the great majority of people who are employed in a given year will be employed in the very same position the next year. This being the case, it becomes important not only to examine the status of minorities and women in the state and local government workforce as a whole, but also to attend closely to the characteristics of a particular subset of employees: those who have been newly hired, whose characteristics can tell us a good deal about what is <u>currently</u> being done to change the composition of the workforce.

Table 3 provides data on the approximately 670,000 state and local government employees who were newly hired in 1980. Of these new hires, only 35.8 percent were white males, well below the 1980 white male percentage of the state and local government workforce (47.7). Thus, almost one of every two state and local government employees, but only about one in three of the new hires, was a white male. Every other group -- white females along with black, Spanish-surnamed, Asian, and Indian males and females -- was better represented among the new hires than in the 1980 state and local government workforce as a whole. In fact, the absolute number of white female new hires exceeded the number of white male new hires, reversing the situation that prevailed in the entire state and local government workforce. More generally, in each racial/ethnic group the ratio of women to men was more favorable among new hires than among carryover employees.

TABLE 3

Composition and Positions of 1980 New Hires

Group	Number	Percentage	% of Higher Positions
White Male	238,689	35.8	38.3
White Female	251,343	37.7	46.2
Black Male	63,644	9.5	3.8
Black Female	60,209	9.0	6.0
Spanish-Surnamed Male	20,121	3.0	1.6
Spanish-Surnamed Female	17,404	2.6	1.2
Asian Male	5,219	0.8	1.2
Asian Female	5,740	0.9	1.2
Indian Male	2,203	0.3	0.2
Indian Female	1,902	0.3	0.2
TOTAL	666,494	100.0	99.9*

*Varies from 100.0 percent due to rounding. Data are from the 1980 source cited in Table 1.

Viewed from this perspective, changes in the composition of the state and local government workforce seem considerably less sluggish than when the focus is on the composition of the state and local workforce as a whole.

Data on the median salaries of new hirees are not available, but we can get some feel for the quality of the positions held by new hirees if we focus on high-ranking positions -- "higher-ranking" in this context referring to positions of an administrative or professional character. According to Table 3, 38.3 percent of the newly hired administrative and professional employees in 1980 were white males, slightly more than the white male share of all new hirees. More strikingly, Table 3 also indicates that almost half (46.2 percent) of the new administrative and professional employees were white females, considerably above the white female share of all new employees (37.7). Thus, almost 85 percent of the newly hired higher-ranking employees were whites, well above the white share of all new hirees (73 percent). It follows that minority hirees were underrepresented among higher-ranking new employees, and what was true of new minority employees in general held for each minority group except Asians, who were disproportionately found among the higher-ranking new employees.

These positional data are encouraging insofar as they relate to the quality of jobs assumed by white females. But for members of minority groups these findings indicate that the positional inferiority so evident in the salary advantage scores reported in Table 2 was not, as of 1980, in the process of being overcome. Members of racial-ethnic minority groups were being hired in relatively large numbers, but the quality of the positions they were filling did not compare favorably to the quality of the positions being filled by white males, let alone white females.

INTERGOVERNMENTAL COMPARISONS, 1975-1978

Do the quantity and quality of the jobs held by minorities and women differ across levels of government? Since the national government has been the leader in promoting equal employment opportunity and affirmative action, we might expect it to have a superior record as an employer of minorities and women. No comparative analyses of the progress of minorities and women in state, county, and municipal governments have yet been undertaken, so we have little to go on in formulating further expectations. We also need to recognize that the data on the state, county, and municipal government workforces are aggregated on a nationwide basis and thus encompass, at each level of government, jurisdictions characterized by vast political, cultural, and socioeconomic

differences. Of course, cities are more likely than counties or
states to have large concentrations of minorities, who can try to
use their political clout to make local governments responsive to
their demands for more and better government jobs. The
evidence in this regard is mixed (e.g., Dye and Renick, 1981;
Eisinger, 1982a; Welch, Karnig, and Eribes, 1983b), but if this
strategy is at all effective then municipalities might be
expected to have better minority employment records than
either state or county governments. County governments have
an image as the last bastions of rural control, minimally
disposed to respond to emerging social forces. Accordingly, we
might expect county governments to have compiled particularly
poor records in the employment of minorities and women.
States are more difficult to characterize because of the great
differences among them in political traditions and in the
political access of minorities and women, but we might
anticipate that they fall into an intermediate position between
city governments on the one hand and county governments on
the other in terms of the progress minorities and women have
made in gaining more and better jobs.

    Again, these expectations are highly tentative, because
the data at our disposal tend to mask varying political, cultural,
and socioeconomic characteristics in individual jurisdictions and
also because these expectations are based upon impressions
rather than systematic evidence from prior studies. The
intergovernmental comparisons undertaken here must thus be
understood as a preliminary mapping operation designed to
isolate gross similarities and differences among federal, state,
county and municipal governments; more finely-grained
intergovernmental comparisons are badly needed, but they will
be difficult to undertake unless and until EEOC's statutory
policy of not making government workforce data available on an
individual jurisdictional basis is reversed.

The Quantitative Dimension
    Table 4 details the racial/ethnic and sexual composition of
the federal, state, county, and municipal government workforces
as of 1975 and 1978. At the federal and municipal levels, white
males in 1978 accounted for 55-60 percent of the workforce, and
white females for appreciably less -- approximately 22 percent
in the federal service and 15 percent in the cities. Altogether,
then, about three workers in four at the federal and municipal
levels were white, with seven or eight of every ten white
workers being males. At the state and county levels, whites
were even more numerically predominant, in both cases
comprising more than 80 percent of the workforce. However, in
both state and county governments the ratio of white males to
white females was much more even than it was in federal or

TABLE 4

Composition of Government Employment at Various Levels, 1975-1978

Group	Federal Government[a] 1975	1978	State Government[b] 1975	1978
White Male	1,371,465 (57.2%)	1,301,949 (55.9%)	779,615 (49.4%)	742,570 (46.1%)
White Female	514,548 (21.5%)	534,214 (22.1%)	555,876 (35.2%)	574,660 (35.7%)
Black Male	218,806 (9.1%)	218,063 (9.0%)	69,847 (4.4%)	88,615 (5.5%)
Black Female	165,384 (6.9%)	176,813 (7.3%)	120,032 (7.6%)	139,904 (8.7%)
Spanish-Surnamed Male	63,172 (2.6%)	64,404 (2.6%)	21,936 (1.4%)	23,745 (1.5%)
Spanish-Surnamed Female	17,617 (0.7%)	20,556 (0.9%)	16,883 (1.1%)	20,470 (1.3%)
Asian Male	16,416 (0.7%)	17,641 (0.7%)	5,054 (0.3%)	8,123 (0.5%)
Asian Female	7,097 (0.3%)	8,666 (0.4%)	4,539 (0.3%)	7,240 (0.4%)
Indian Male	11,572 (0.5%)	13,328 (0.6%)	2,855 (0.2%)	3,507 (0.2%)
Indian Female	9,886 (0.4%)	12,517 (0.5%)	2,167 (0.1%)	2,909 (0.2%)
TOTAL	2,395,963 (99.9%)	2,418,151 (100.0%)	1,578,804 (100.0%)	1,611,743 (100.1%)

Group	County Government[b] 1975	1978	City Government[b] 1975	1978
White Male	349,427 (43.9%)	415,219 (41.4%)	746,105 (59.3%)	849,610 (58.3%)
White Female	308,427 (38.8%)	401,089 (40.0%)	746,105 (59.3%)	216,894 (14.9%)
Black Male	40,234 (5.1%)	52,626 (5.2%)	176,099 (14.0%)	200,769 (13.5%)
Black Female	55,493 (7.0%)	73,092 (7.3%)	84,155 (6.7%)	94,011 (6.5%)
Spanish-Surnamed Male	16,510 (2.1%)	22,807 (2.3%)	51,733 (4.1%)	60,846 (4.2%)
Spanish-Surnamed Female	14,927 (1.9%)	21,553 (2.1%)	12,941 (1.0%)	16,044 (1.1%)
Asian Male	3,325 (0.4%)	5,107 (0.5%)	4,127 (0.3%)	8,095 (0.6%)
Asian Female	4,139 (0.5%)	6,856 (0.7%)	2,894 (0.2%)	5,348 (0.4%)
Indian Male	1,491 (0.2%)	2,666 (0.3%)	2,014 (0.2%)	3,850 (0.3%)
Indian Female	1,211 (0.2%)	2,207 (0.2%)	447 (0.0%)	1,080 (0.1%)
TOTAL	795,112 (100.1%)*	1,003,222 (100.0)	1,257,805 (99.9%)*	1,456,547 (100.2%)*

[a] Data are from Civil Service Commission, Bureau of Manpower Information Systems, Minority Group Employment in the Federal Government, 1975 (Washington, D.C.: Government Printing Office, 1975); and Office of Personnel Management, Equal Employment Opportunity Statistics, 1978 (Washington, D.C.: Government Printing Office, 1978).

[b] Data are from EEOC, Minorities and Women in State and Local Government, 1975 (Washington, D.C.: Government Printing Office, 1977); and EEOC, Minorities and Women in State and Local Government, 1978 (Washington, D.C.: Government Printing Office, 1980).

municipal governments. In state governments more than four of every ten white employees were women, and in county governments the male-female split was almost 50-50.

In this sense, federal and municipal governments stood out fairly clearly on the one hand from state and county governments on the other. Following the same pattern, the proportion of black male employees was substantially larger at the federal and municipal levels (9.0 percent and 13.5 percent, respectively) than it was at either the state or the county level (5.5 percent and 5.2 percent, respectively), while black women did somewhat better in state and county governments. The same basic pattern held for Spanish-surnamed, Asian American, and American Indian employees as well, although these trends were often not very pronounced because of the small sizes of the groups involved.

As of 1978, then, there was a "male bias" in federal and municipal employment to an extent unmatched at the state or county level. We do not pretend to have a comprehensive explanation for this, but we can mention some possibilities that seem worth considering. The demographic composition of the various levels of government may vary as a reflection of functional differences among levels of government. Some of the primary functions performed by local governments, e.g., police protection, fire fighting, and sanitation, have traditionally been monopolized by males, presumably because of the danger or physical demands associated with these jobs. Women have made some significant inroads into these functional areas in recent years, but these are and will presumably remain male-dominated functions.

This functional interpretation certainly should not be discounted, but neither should it be accepted as a full explanation of the numerical predominance of males in the federal and municipal workforces. In the first place, even though it is beyond the scope of this paper to detail the racial/ethnic and sexual composition of government workers in the various functional fields, we can report that in 1978 the female percentage of the municipal workforce was lower than the female percentage of the state and county workforces even within the very same functional areas and even in functional areas where danger and physical demands should not be a consideration. Moreover, the functional explanation cannot account for the relatively low female percentages of federal government employees, for the federal service is much less dominated than municipal governments by such stereotypically "male" occupations as policing and fire-fighting.

Another line of explanation would focus on the "tipping" phenomenon that has often been observed in studies of racial patterns in school enrollments, residential segregation, and the like (see, e.g., Schelling, 1972). The basic idea of a tipping interpretation would be that as an out-group comes to dominate positions previously held by the in-group, members of the in-group choose to seek employment elsewhere. In other words, once a certain point is reached the process accelerates itself. If that is true (and we can only speculate about the applicability of this idea to the problem at hand), then the explanation for racial patterns in employment in various job groups, agencies, and so on would lie at least in part in the realm of labor supply rather than demand.

A third possibility stems from the fact that, as we had anticipated, the minority share of the government workforce was higher at the federal and municipal levels than it was at the state and county levels. This is consistent with the notion that responsiveness to racial/ethnic group demands has historically been greatest at the very top and the very bottom of the American federal system -- embodied in the case of employment by the federal government's role in spearheading equal employment opportunity and affirmative action programs and by urban political machines' vast patronage systems. Such responsiveness to minority demands has, however, apparently not been complemented by a corresponding attentiveness to nonracially-based uses of public employment. As a consequence, the interests of racial/ethnic minorities have sometimes, whether inadvertently or not, ended up being played off against the interests of women. Just as Sigelman (1976) concluded that female state and local government employees tended to be most underrepresented in states where minorities were best represented, so it would seem that female government employees are at least numerous at the very levels of government where minorities are most numerous.

Although we wish to be very circumspect in interpreting trends over the brief 1975-1978 period, inspection of Table 4 indicates that white males, who in 1975 held a majority of the jobs at the federal and municipal levels and a plurality of the jobs at the state and county levels, continued to do so in 1978, but by a narrower margin than they had in 1975. That is, at all four levels of government the percentage of white males declined between 1975 and 1978. At the federal and state levels, the absolute number of white males decreased, while at the county and municipal levels the number of white males increased, but less rapidly than the workforce as a whole.

In examining the issue of which groups benefitted from the growth of government employment, the picture is less clear. All groups except white males were employed in greater numbers in 1978 at all levels of government than they had been in 1975. By a small margin, white females appear to have fared the best in terms of the growth in their percentage of the workforce across jurisdictions. The pattern for blacks was less consistent. At the state level the proportion of jobs held by black men and women increased by 1.1 percent, while at the remaining levels of government this proportion held constant or varied slightly upwards or downwards. In every case, though, the absolute number of blacks grew from 1975 to 1978.

In sum, between 1975 and 1978 the share of positions held by females and minority group members at every level of government increased and the proportion of positions held by white males decreased. A one to three percent drop in the proportion of jobs held by white males represents a fairly large-scale change over a three-year timespan, leading us to conclude that on the quantitative dimension the trend during the mid-1970s was in the direction of a more broadly representative public service at all levels of American government.

The Qualitative Dimension

Tables 5 and 6 relate to the quality of the jobs held by members of each group at each level of government. Table 5 is not directly comparable to Table 6, for while data on state, county, and municipal employees' median yearly salaries are available, the same is not true of federal employees. Reporting for federal employees is in terms of grades in one of the many different federal employee classification systems, which cannot be reduced to a common denominator. Accordingly, the data in Table 5 are only for General Schedule federal employees, who comprise more than half of all federal civilian employees. Moreover, these data, unlike the data given in Table 6, are median grades on the 1-18 scale employed in the General Schedule system rather than median salaries. The "advantage index" scores for federal workers were calculated by dividing the median GS level of the members of a given group by the median GS level of white males during the same year.

As these tables indicate, only Asian males and (in county and municipal governments) Asian females fared better than white males in terms of median GS grades or salary levels. More strikingly, however, in both 1975 and 1978 at all four levels of government and in every racial/ethnic group, average job quality was considerably higher for men than it was for women. Again, the special nature of the data for federal employees does not permit any precise comparisons to be made, but the male-female GS grade differentials presented in Table 5 are of the same general order of magnitude as the salary differentials presented in Table 6.

The gap between men and women on the qualitative dimension was not only very sizeable, but also quite persistent. Looking across the columns in Table 6, we see that the standing of minorities and women relative to white males improved very

TABLE 5

Federal Employee Median GS Level and Advantage Index
by Group--1975 and 1978

Group	1975		1978	
White Male	10.5	(1.00)	8.7	(1.00)
White Female	4.5	(.43)	4.8	(.55)
Black Male	6.0	(.57)	6.4	(.74)
Black Female	4.3	(.41)	4.6	(.53)
Spanish-Surnamed Male	6.6	(.63)	8.2	(.94)
Spanish-Surnamed Female	3.9	(.37)	4.3	(.49)
Asian Male	10.4	(.99)	10.6	(1.22)
Asian Female	4.9	(.47)	5.8	(.67)
Indian Male	6.2	(.59)	7.0	(.80)
Indian Female	3.6	(.34)	3.8	(.44)
TOTAL	6.9	(.66)	8.0	(.92)

Source: Table 4.

little, if at all, between 1975 and 1978. The exception in this regard was the federal government, where the median GS grade of employees in every category except white males rose from 1975 to 1978. In every racial/ethnic group the gap between males and females actually widened in absolute dollar terms between 1975 and 1978 in state and municipal governments. In county governments the absolute dollar gap widened for white females but closed slightly in each of the remaining categories.

Progress for minority males was mixed. At the federal level there were increases in the median GS level of males in every minority group, and the advantage ratios for minority males increased markedly. At the state and municipal levels, all categories of minority males except Asians gained modestly relative to white males. Asian males, who began with a substantial advantage, fell back slightly at the state level but held their place at the municipal level. However, at the county level, again with the exception of Asians, minority males remained constant or lost salary ground to white males.

At all levels of government, women in 1978 were still at a disadvantage to men in terms of the quality of the positions they held. Except among Asians, females invariably rated poorly on the salary advantage index. In 1978, the highest non-Asian female advantage index was actually lower than the lowest minority male advantage index at each level of government.

TABLE 6

Employee Median Salary and Advantage Index, by Group, Various Levels of Government, 1975 and 1978

Group	State Government 1975		State Government 1978		County Government 1975		County Government 1978		City Government 1975		City Government 1978	
White Male	$11,046	(1.00)	$13,319	(1.00)	$10,920	(1.00)	$12,402	(1.00)	$12,349	(1.00)	$14,282	(1.00)
White Female	8,330	(.75)	10,104	(.76)	7,978	(.73)	9,291	(.75)	8,494	(.69)	9,991	(.70)
Black Male	8,336	(.75)	10,190	(.77)	8,908	(.82)	9,977	(.80)	9,733	(.79)	11,251	(.79)
Black Female	7,575	(.69)	9,233	(.69)	7,841	(.72)	9,304	(.75)	8,835	(.72)	9,868	(.69)
Spanish-Surnamed Male	9,415	(.85)	11,907	(.89)	9,965	(.91)	11,272	(.91)	9,682	(.78)	11,691	(.82)
Spanish-Surnamed Female	7,427	(.67)	9,240	(.69)	7,766	(.71)	9,373	(.76)	8,114	(.66)	9,303	(.65)
Asian Male	15,428	(1.40)	17,389	(1.31)	13,866	(1.27)	15,861	(1.28)	13,999	(1.13)	16,185	(1.13)
Asian Female	9,901	(.90)	11,854	(.89)	10,378	(.95)	12,856	(1.04)	11,083	(.90)	12,709	(.89)
Indian Male	10,180	(.92)	12,712	(.95)	9,987	(.91)	11,005	(.89)	10,961	(.89)	13,221	(.93)
Indian Female	7,839	(.71)	9,879	(.74)	7,680	(.70)	9,063	(.73)	8,358	(.68)	10,270	(.72)
TOTAL	9,404	(.85)	11,382	(.85)	9,165	(.84)	10,546	(.85)	10,941	(.89)	13,360	(.94)

Source: See Table 4.

So it is fair to say that during the 1975-1978 period males retained their salary advantage over females. Minority males, with the exception of Asians, continued to trail white males, but females in each group were much farther behind.

In sum, while there was considerable variability among the four levels of government on the quantitative dimension of minority and female employment, there was an overriding sameness about the quality of minority and female positions in the federal, state, county, and municipal workforces. At no level of government was the quality of the positions held by white males matched, or even approached, by any other group -- the lone exception being the tiny contingent of Asian Americans. Moreover, at no level of government was the quality of the positions held by males matched, or even approached, by females of the same racial/ethnic group. So while the quantity of minority and female public service jobs varied considerably from one level of government to another, the relatively poor quality of the positions held by minorities and especially by women would be seen at all levels of government, without exception.

CONCLUSION

Between 1973 and 1980, minorities and women did make measurable, even impressive, progress in gaining jobs in state and local government. White males bore the brunt of this progress, their relative share of the government workforce falling by some seven percent in seven years and the absolute number of positions they occupied declining by more than 180,000. As of 1980 every other group commanded a larger proportional share and a greater absolute number of jobs in state and local government than it had in 1973. The biggest "winners" were white females, although by 1980 they had still not come close to the white male share of state and local government jobs.

In terms of the qualitative dimension, the 1973-1980 period witnessed very little movement. Every group except Asian males began the period at a salary disadvantage to white males, and every group except Asian males ended the period at a salary disadvantage to white males. Women in every racial/ethnic category began the period at a substantial salary disadvantage to men in the same racial/ethnic category and ended the period in the very same position.

These trends showed up most clearly with respect to employees who were newly hired as of 1980. These new employees were much more representative, in a demographic sense, than the state and local government workforce as a whole. But with the notable exception of white females, the positions that minorities and women were being hired to fill did not compare favorably to the positions occupied by newly hired white males.

Prior to undertaking this study, we suspected that the federal government and municipal government might have established better records as employers of minorities than either state or county governments. This was borne out in our analysis of the quantitative dimension of employment. However, we also noted that women accounted for a larger share of the state and county than of the federal and municipal workforces. So women fared worst, quantitatively, precisely where minorities fared best. Thus we see once again that it is misleading to refer to "minorities and women" as a single group that gains or loses from particular personnel policies. In accommodating the needs and demands of one of these groups, government agencies may well end up being unresponsive to the needs and demands of the other -- or, to return to the "tipping" idea, white women may try to avoid employment situations dominated by racial minorities. Finally, we have seen that even though the federal and municipal levels of government have done the best job of hiring large numbers of minority group members, they have been no more successful than state or county governments at establishing minorities in positions comparable to those occupied by whites. In fact, there is little room to choose among the various levels of government in terms of their performance on the qualitative dimension of the employment of either minorities or women. If the expansion of the sheer number of minorities and women in the public sector workforce was the primary accomplishment of equal employment opportunity and affirmative action programs during the 1970s, then it should be equally obvious that the expansion of the number of minorities and women in higher quality positions poses the foremost challenge of the 1980s.

REFERENCES

Benokraitis, Nijole V., and Joe R. Feagin. 1978. Affirmative Action and Equal Opportunity: Action, Inaction, Reaction. Boulder: Westview Press.

Borcher, Rita R. 1982. "Does tradition affect affirmative action results? How Pennsylvania achieved changes at the middle management level." Public Administration Review 42 (September/October): 475-478.

Cayer, N. Joseph, and Lee Sigelman. 1980. "Minorities and women in state and local government: 1973-1975." Public Administration Review 40 (September/October 1980): 433-450.

Civil Service Commission, Bureau of Manpower Information Systems. 1975. Minority Group Employment in the Federal Government. Washington, D.C.: Government Printing Office.

Dye, Thomas, and James Renick. 1981. "Political Power and City Jobs: Determinants of Minority Employment." Social Science Quarterly 62 (September): 475-486.

Eisinger, Peter K. 1982a. "Black Employment in Municipal Jobs: The Impact of Black Political Power." American Political Science Review 76 (June): 380-392.

_____ 1982. "The Economic Conditions of Black Employment in Municipal Bureaucracies." American Journal of Political Science 26 (November): 754-771.

Elling, Richard C. 1983. "State bureaucracies." in (eds.Virginia Gray, Herbert Jacob, and Kenneth N. Vines.) Politics in the American States: A Comparative Analysis, fourth edition. Boston: Little, Brown. pp. 244-283.

Equal Employment Opportunity Commission. 1974a. Affirmative Action and Equal Employment: A Guidebook for Employers. Vol. 1. Washington, D.C.: EEOC.

_____ 1974b. Minorities and Women in State and Local Government, 1973. Washington, D.C.: Government Printing Office.

_____ 1977. Minorities and Women in State and Local Government, 1975. Washington, D.C.: Government Printing Office.

_____ 1980. Minorities and Women in State and Local Government, 1978. Washington, D.C.: Government Printing Office.

_____ 1982. Job Patterns for Minorities and Women in State and Local Government, 1980. Washington, D.C.: Government Printing Office.

Hall, Grace, and Alan Saltzstein. 1977. "Equal Employment Opportunity for Minorities in Municipal Government." Social Science Quarterly 57 (March): 864-872.

Henderson, Lenneal J. 1978. "The Impact of the Equal Employment Opportunity Act of 1972 on Employment Opportunities for Women and Minorities in Municipal Government." Policy Studies Journal 7 (Winter): 234-239.

Hutchins, Matthew, and Lee Sigelman. 1981. "Black employment in state and local governments: a comparative analysis." Social Science Quarterly 62 (March 1981): 79-87.

Kranz, Harry. 1976. The Participatory Bureaucracy. Lexington, Mass.: D.C. Heath and Co.

Meier, Kenneth J. 1978. "Constraints on Affirmative Action." Policy Studies Journal 7 (Winter): 208-213.

Office of Personnel Management. 1978. Equal Employment Opportunity Statistics. Washington, D.C.: Government Printing Office.

Rose, Winfield H., and Tiang Ping Chia. 1978. "The Impact of the Equal Employment Opportunity Act of 1972 on Black Employment in the Federal Service: A Preliminary Analysis." Public Administration Review 38 (May/June): 245-251.

Schelling, Thomas C. 1972. "A Process of Residential Segregation: A Neighborhood Tipping." Pp. 157-184 in Anthony H. Pascal (ed.), Racial Discrimination in Economic Life. Lexington, Mass.: D.C. Heath.

Sigelman, Lee. 1976. "The Curious Case of Women in State and Local Government." Social Science Quarterly 57 (March): 591-604.

_____, and Albert K. Karnig. 1977. "Black Education and Bureaucratic Employment." Social Science Quarterly 58 (March): 858-863.

Smith, Russell L. 1980. "Representative Bureaucracy: A Research Note on Demographic Representation in State Bureaucracies." Review of Public Personnel Administration 1: 1-13.

Welch, Susan, Albert K. Karnig, and Richard A. Eribes. 1983a. "Changes in Hispanic Local Public Employment in the

Southwest." <u>Western Political Quarterly</u> 36 (December): 660-673.

_____ 1983b. "Correlates of Women's Employment in Local Governments." <u>Urban Affairs Quarterly</u> 18 (June): 551-564.

Peter K. Eisinger

The Impact of Economic Transformations
on Black Municipal Employment

One of the places in which effects of the economic transformations currently taking place in American society are clearly felt is the municipal public sector workforce. The most basic impact of these various economic forces is to set in motion a chain of events that leads to the expansion or contraction of the number of public employees in any given city. As a consequence, opportunities for employment are created or restricted. These changes in the opportunity structure, I will argue, tend to affect various social groups in the society differently. For a variety of reasons discussed below, this is particularly true for blacks. This chapter seeks to explore some of the effects of certain public and private economic trends on shifts in levels of black municipal employment in the last decade.

Economic Transformation in American Cities

Certain economic changes that affect American cities have been under way for several decades. Perhaps the most important of these -- and the one of longest duration -- is the regional shift in patterns of urbanization. One part of this trend is the decline since around 1950 of Northeastern and Midwestern central cities, produced by the relocation in the dispersed metropolis and to other parts of the country of population and business activity. Population decline is closely linked to local economic deterioration (JCPS, 1982: 46). The effects of this economic vortex are felt on the municipal public sector: as a city loses its people and businesses, it seeks ways to adjust its expenditures to its diminished tax base (Levine, et al., 1982). Since most cities spend between two-thirds and three-quarters of their revenues on personnel, the pool of municipal employees is an obvious target for contraction.

112

A second aspect of the regional shift is the growth of Southern and Western cities. These places have had to grapple with the problems of rampant growth, the burdens of which have been softened, perhaps, by the relative prosperity of their situation. Houston, with its 29 percent growth rate over the last decade, Austin (37%), Charlotte (30%), and Little Rock (20%) exemplify this pattern.

Among the problems induced by rapid growth is the need to service a vastly larger population. To compound the pressures of sheer population growth, many of the migrants to the warm regions come from northern cities, where people take for granted an array of municipal services not typically found in the Sunbelt (Lupsha and Siembieda, 1977). One consequence of such forces is the rapid expansion of the public sector workforce in growing cities. Houston, for example, hired over 5000 workers between 1973 and 1980, enlarging its workforce from 11,839 to 17,134. Charlotte's workforce went from 3300 to nearly 3900 in the same period, while Miami added more than 600 people, bringing its total number of employees to 4000. Nationally, municipal public employment is no longer a growth industry, but these few regionally limited areas are exceptions. Here employment opportunities are generated for workers at all skill levels and from all social groups. Occasionally, hiring needs are so great that local markets cannot easily provide the workers, necessitating recruiting trips outside the region.

Related to the decline of the Frostbelt central city as a prime economic locus is the transformation of the American economy from its historic manufacturing base to one built increasingly on service and high technology. Competition from abroad, out-moded American production methods, the attraction of investment to new high growth industries and shifting consumer demands have combined to devastate local economies built on heavy industry. For some cities the losses of manufacturing jobs have been dramatic. In the relatively short period from 1972 to 1977, for example, Philadelphia lost nearly 45,000 such jobs, while Pittsburgh lost 23,000. Akron lost almost 12 percent of its manufacturing jobs, Buffalo 8 percent and New Orleans 14 percent (U.S. Bureau of the Census, 1980, Table 1). Some labor economists have argued that with the loss of jobs in the traditional manufacturing occupations in the private sector, the public sector has been cast as an increasingly important source of urban employment (Grosskopf, 1981: 48).

Two other economic forces are of more recent origin, but both affect the urban public sector. One is the cycle of recession and inflation of the last 10 years that helped to produce persistently high unemployment rates toward the end of the decade; the other is the decline of federal intergovernmental aid to the cities.

During the 1970s real economic growth declined in comparison with the rate over the two previous decades, and the Consumer Price Index rose in the 10-year period by 112 percent, far outstripping the inflation rates of 20 percent and 31 percent for 1950s and 1960s, respectively (Sawhill, 1982: 34). In conjunction with these problems unemployment rose to what were heretofore record post-Depression levels: average unemployment over the decade was 6.2 percent, compared with averages of 4.5 and 4.8 percent for the two prior periods (Sawhill, 1982). Many cities averaged double digit unemployment after 1975, well before the national figure reached those levels in the early 1980s. Detroit, Oakland, Pontiac, East St. Louis, and Berkeley, for example, were among those places with average annual unemployment rates over 10 percent for the 1975-1979 period (BLS, annual).

Unemployment produces at least two problems for the public sector workforce. First, tax revenues decline, both those sensitive to earnings and spendings, such as local sales and payroll taxes and those which tend to lag behind other economic trends such as property taxes. This means there is less to spend on local public services. A second problem is that many of the unemployed, shutout of the private sector by lack of training or opportunity, now look toward the city for jobs.[1]

The ability of the city to respond to rising unemployment, however, has been substantially weakened by the decline in federal fiscal assistance. The major effect of federal grants to lower level governments is to increase their spending on personnel (ACIR, 1977; Ashenfelter, 1977). Federal grants to municipalities, measured either in per capita terms or as a percentage of local revenues, increased steadily after the passage of the Great Society programs in the 1960s. But federal aid reached a peak at the mid-point of the Carter presidency in 1978 and began to decline thereafter (Reischauer, 1981). Much of the decline was in fact due to the cessation of programs specifically aimed at increasing or stabilizing local public sector workforce. These programs included the Public Service Employment component of CETA and Anti-Recession Fiscal Assistance, known as countercyclical revenue sharing. Both programs were targeted at areas of high unemployment.

To summarize, a variety of economic transformations, ranging from population shifts and the long term shift to a post-industrial, dispersed metropolitan economy to changing patterns of intergovernmental fiscal assistance and high local unemployment have converged in recent years on the central city. Not all cities, of course, have suffered in the face of these various economic forces: one city's bust may be another's boom. Thus, cities across the nation have experienced these economic changes quite differently.

The effects of these transformations may be seen, among other places, on the local public sector payroll. In general, we would predict that the size of a city's municipal workforce will respond over time to economic influences, contracting under economic duress and expanding under conditions of affluence. Moreover, we may also predict that black employment levels in the city service will be particularly affected over time by these economic forces, both for better and for worse. That is to say, black fortunes in the public sector will be affected disproportionately compared to those of whites by both expansions and contractions of the workforce produced by economic influences.

Under conditions of prosperity, according to this argument, blacks will tend to make great strides in public sector employment. In part, the prevailing sense of security and abundance generated in a city by economic good times will make possible a more generous allocation of public goods, including city jobs. Just as scarcity is likely to produce sharp struggle among groups, so abundance may be expected to diminish intergroup competition as well as pressures on those responsible for allocatory functions. Politically weaker groups will stand to benefit in a healthy economy.

In addition, more blacks than whites prefer work in the public sector to that in the private economy and will tend to gravitate in disproportionate numbers toward expanded opportunities in city employment (on favorable black attitudes toward the public sector, see Frederickson, 1967; Barger, 1976). Conversely, the good jobs being generated by a healthy private sector economy will tend disproportionately to absorb available white labor, lessening racial competition for city work.

Finally, expansion of the public sector, especially if it is rapid, often requires casting a wider recruitment net, pulling in people outside of the usual labor pool.[2]

Economic bad times may be expected to have quite different employment ramifications. Since the burdens of scarcity have historically fallen more heavily on blacks, the costs of diminishing public employment opportunities, may be argued, will not be equitably shared by the races. Public employee cutbacks that result from persistent economic troubles in the private sector or diminishing intergovernmental aid are likely, under certain circumstances, to fall most heavily on black workers.

Black city employees are more vulnerable to layoffs particularly, for as a group they have less seniority than their white counterparts. Unless steps are taken to mitigate the effects of reverse seniority,[3] affirmative action gains can easily vanish in retrenchment. Case studies show how devastating the problems can be. In Cincinnati, for example, layoffs in the mid-

1970s caused 13 percent of black males in public employment to lose their jobs, compared to only 3.2 percent of white males (Thomas, 1978). In the great New York City fiscal crisis 35 percent of black workers lost their jobs, compared to only 22 percent of white workers (NYC, 1976).

Blacks are also put in special jeopardy in hard times because they tend to be concentrated in agencies and job titles considered less essential to the running of the city. Labor-intensive departments (streets, parks) and social services (welfare, housing, community development), where most blacks work, are more likely to face cuts than financial administration departments, economic development agencies, or the mayor's own office, where blacks tend to be underrepresented. Furthermore, most blacks are situated in low-skill occupations, which, in hard times, are seen as dispensable.

Let us turn now to an effort to test these arguments. Do the various economic forces in fact constrict black opportunities over time? If they do so, which are the more important: the long-term, intractable structural forces, such as the flight from Frostbelt cities and the shift to a post-industrial economy, or the relatively short-run factors that may be altered by public policies, such as high unemployment and reduced federal aid?

Black Employment Data and Basic Trends

Data on minority employment in municipal government from a sample of 34 cities provides the means to assess the degree to which economic forces affect black public sector opportunities over time. Black employment data are compiled by individual cities under the terms of the Equal Employment Opportunity Act of 1972. Such data are part of a comprehensive breakdown of each city's workforce by race, sex, functional category, occupational status and salary, collected and sent annually to the U.S. Equal Employment Opportunity Commission in Washington. Since the terms of the law forbid the federal commission from releasing these data except as national aggregates, individual city data must be collected from the personnel departments of the cities themselves. Figures on black employment were gathered over several years for 1973 (the baseline year), 1978 and 1980.

The data used in the present analysis do not include education personnel, CETA workers or less than full-time employees. In some cities non-mayoral agencies -- that is, those with authority independent of the local chief executive -- are not included in the official tabulations, but this varies from city to city. In general, the data represent a census of all full-time employees in agencies ranging from financial administration to police and fire, from streets to parks and recreation, from housing and community development to sanitation and corrections, among others.

The 34 cities represent a distillation of two merged samples, one of all cities over 250,000, the other a supplementary random sample of cities between 50,000 and 250,000. Of the original cities sampled only 51 of those 85 that responded initially met the threshold criterion of a 10 percent or higher black population. Of these 51 cities, only 34 were able to supply complete data on minority employment for all three years requested.[4] Since the central purpose of this analysis is to examine black employment change, the inquiry had to be limited to this smaller group. Thus, the sample is not a random one.

As might be expected, the racial composition of the sample cities is different from the national urban pattern: In 1980 blacks made up an average of 32.7 percent of the sample city populations, compared to 22.5 percent of the central city populations in all 323 standard Metropolitan Statistical Areas (U.S. Bureau of the Census, 1982: 49). The sample is weighted in favor of large cities, but size is not significantly correlated with any of the variables used in the present analysis, either in various multiple regressions or in any bivariate relationship. Eighteen of the cities are located in the South, Southwest and California. The remaining 16 are located mainly in the Northeast and Great Lakes region.

Trends during the decade show that the proportion of blacks among all employees of the 34 cities rose slightly from an average of 26.7 percent in 1973 to 29.3 percent in 1980. Growth in the percentage of blacks was more pronounced in select occupational categories at the top of the authority and prestige scale: the percentage of black administrators advanced from 9.1 to 15.5 percent in that period, while the black share of professional jobs moved from 11.3 percent to 17.8.

Calculated as a ratio of their percentage of the local population, blacks are on the average slightly overrepresented on city workforces, but they lost ground during the decade. Taking a score of 100 as an index of perfect proportional representation on the workforce, the average "fair share" score declined from 109.7 in 1973 to 102.2 in 1980. In other words, a smaller proportion of the black population in the sample cities was employed by city government in 1980 than in 1973. At the two high occupational levels, however, there were real gains (indicating that the loss of ground came through contraction of lower level jobs). Although blacks were substantially underrepresented as administrators and professionals, even at the end of the decade, the average fair share scores in both cases advanced significantly. The average administrator score went from 30.4 to 47.6, while the average professional fair share score rose from 41 to 55.7.

The increase in fair share scores for high-level occupations and the decrease for the workforces as a whole suggest that the pool of black municipal employees is becoming increasingly professionalized. Although a decreasing proportion of the black population was finding work with the city, the losses of black jobs were entirely concentrated among lower-level occupations.

These aggregate patterns of change in black employment mask some great variations among the sample cities. While the proportion of blacks on the workforce was growing in East St. Louis by nearly 32 percentage points in the 1970s and in Houston by 11, other cities were registering losses. The percentage of black city workers in Pontiac declined by 6 points; in Beaumont, Texas, by almost 11 points. Cincinnati, Tulsa, Toledo, and Durham showed virtually no change over the decade. Fair share change scores ranged between -53 (Beaumont) to +50 (Berkeley). Even more extreme variations are found at the administrator and professional levels. The city-by-city variations provide the context for the analysis that follows. The trends are summarized in Table 1.

Table 1

Trends in Black Municipal Employment, 1973-1980, in 34 Cities

Average change in percent black, total workforce	2.6*
Average change in percent black, administrators only	6.4*
Average change in percent black, professionals only	6.5*
Range of percent change scores, total workforce	-10.7 to +31.7*
Range of percent change scores, administrators only	-7.2 to +40.1*
Range of percent change scores, professionals only	-13.2 to +31.3*
Average change in fair share score, total workforce	-4.2**
Average change in fair share score, administrators only	16.2**
Average change in fair share score, professionals only	14.0**
Range of fair share change scores, total workforce	-53 to + 50**
Range of fair share change scores, administrators only	-36 to +127**
Range of fair share change scores, professionals only	-28 to + 88**

* Figures are percentage points.
** Figures are the difference between the fair share score in 1973 and that in 1980. The fair share index is calculated by dividing the percentage on the workforce by the percentage black in the city's population.

Economic Transformation and Black City Employment Change: A Regression Analysis

If we accept population growth as a sign of a city's relative economic prosperity, then the predicted connection between local economic vitality and the public sector is solidly established. The correlation (r) between the rate of population increase and growth of the public sector workforce is a robust .65.[5] Conversely, cities which lose population tend to experience shrinkage of their public workforce. How are black opportunities for public employment affected in a labor market affected by these economic forces?

Several multiple regression models were run using various measures of black employment change as dependent variables. Regional patterns of urban growth and decline were measured by population change over the decade of the 1970s. Among Frostbelt cities 15 out of 16 lost population in these years, while 15 out of the 18 Sunbelt cities in the sample gained population, making this variable a reasonably accurate reflection of regional patterns of urbanization. Population growth is negatively related to high unemployment levels a the -.65 level. The state of the local economy was also measured by the rate of per capita revenue growth during the years of the study period, 1973 to 1980. The transformation to a post-industrial economy, another long-term factor, is indicated by the decline of local manufacturing jobs. (Without knowing whether lost manufacturing jobs were replaced locally by service and technical positions, we cannot know whether a city's economy is experiencing transformation to a post-industrial state or whether it is simply collapsing. But relative rates of manufacturing loss provide a good measure of how different cities have borne the costs of national economic transformation.) As Table 2 shows, growth of manufacturing employment is related to a moderate level to population growth, but manufacturing, we may assume, is not the primary base on which the new urban economies are being constructed. Data on manufacturing are from the 1972-1977 period, as collected and published by the Department of Commerce.

Short-term economic factors -- that is, those that are relatively recent and capable of reversal -- include local unemployment and the shift in federal aid patterns. Unemployment is measured as a five-year average and as a dynamic variable capturing change between 1977 and 1979. Missing data for a few cities for a few years prior to 1977 precluded using change data over a long period of time. Yearly unemployment averages for each city, compiled by the Bureau of Labor Statistics, were used to compute both the five-year average and the change data.

Between 1977 and 1979 all but three cities showed decreases in their unemployment rates. A high decrease in unemployment -- that is, a relatively large improvement in the local job situation -- is associated, not surprisingly, with prior growth of manufacturing jobs in the 1972-1977 period and an increase in per capita revenues over the decade.

Federal aid to local governments also underwent changes in the 1970s, but the shift was not universal. In general, the rate of federal fiscal assistance began to decline after 1978.

Table 2

Intercorrelations Among the Independent
Economic Transformation Variables (r)

	a.	b.	c.	d.	e.	f.
a. population growth, 1970-1980	--					
b. per capita local revenue growth, 1973-1980	.08	--				
c. growth of manufacturing jobs, 1972-1977	.23	.21	--			
d. average employment rate, 1975-1979	-.64	.02	.29	--		
e. increase in unemployment, 1977-1979	.07	-.30	-.45	-.44	--	
f. growth in per capita federal revenues, 1973-1980	.04	.58	.35	.23	-.40	--
g. growth of federal revenue as a percentage of local revenue, 1973-1980	.01	.38	.18	-.10	-.21	.59

While the federal contribution as a percent of local revenues was smaller in 1980 than in 1973 in only six of the cities, the remaining sample cities display quite variable levels of growth of dependence over the seven-year period. Cincinnati, for example, showed an increase of more than 18 percentage points, while the smallest growth of one percentage point was registered by Austin, Texas. East St. Louis lost more than 11 points in these years. On the average federal aid accounted for an additional 6.6 percent of total local revenues in 1980 compared to 1973.

The shift in federal aid is also measured by percentage changes in per capita receipts from Washington between 1973 and 1980. All but three cities showed increases by this measure; rates of growth among the remaining cities varied enormously (from 4 percent to 903 percent).

Table 2 suggests that there is some degree of multicollinearity among the independent variables. In most cases the intercorrelations are not high enough to be of concern. It is the case, however, that two key variables, average unemployment rate and population growth, are strongly inversely related. But since unemployment levels are theoretically amenable to policy manipulation, while population growth or decline is far less so, the two variables, despite their close relationship, are included in the regressions. Each represents a different order of problem for the local political economy.

Growth in total per capita revenues is a measure not only of intergovernmental receipts but also of the health of the local economy and the political willingness to tap it. It is strongly related to growth of federal aid. But since the latter is clearly only one aspect of the former (and in a static sense a modest one, accounting on the average in 1980 for only 20 percent of the revenues of these cities) both variables are included in the regressions.

The first regression, Model I, in which the dependent variable is the growth in the percent of blacks on the workforce, is not very powerful. It produces an R^2 of only .23. The most important independent variables are the unemployment measures, although they are not statistically significant. Nevertheless, as local unemployment rises, so too does the proportion of blacks on the city workforce, a sign that black workers, either thrown out of work or forced to seek employment in a more competitive private labor market, turn to a relatively receptive public sector. The association of a decline in manufacturing jobs and an increase in black public employment provides additional support for the notion that contraction of the private sector drives blacks to seek work in the public sector and that city hall has been responsive.

An alternative hypothesis regarding the effects of high unemployment on black employment finds no support here, namely that high levels of joblessness should restrict black opportunities in the public sector by causing declines in local revenues, which in turn lead to layoffs of city workers, especially vulnerable minorities.

The second model, in which the fair share score change serves as the dependent variable, offers a richer context for exploring black employment progress. Here nearly half the variance in growth rates (R^2 = .46) is explained. Population growth is overwhelmingly the single most important independent variable. In addition, note the strong positive association of black progress with per capita revenue growth and the negative association with black population growth. Combined, these findings militate strongly for the view that real black progress -- that is, a situation in which an increasingly large proportion of the local black population is employed by the city -- occurs under conditions of relative economic prosperity. It is true, however, that when all other variables are controlled, unemployment is still related to higher levels of black penetration of the public sector. Unemployment still acts to push black workers toward city jobs, and city hall in turn is more receptive in growing cities.

We may conclude that black employment opportunities in city work are expanding faster in the growing cities of the West and the old South than in the northeastern centers of black urban concentration. Blacks are comparatively recent migrants to Sunbelt cities, reversing a nearly century-long migration stream to northern cities, once regarded as places of genuine opportunity.

It is striking finally to observe that increases in per capita federal aid are not associated with black employment progress. Presumably, such assistance is more heavily weighted in favor of the depressed cities of the Frostbelt, not the places with relatively vibrant local economies. In any event such aid is not, apparently, being translated into increased numbers of city jobs for blacks.

Several additional regressions were run in which black employment at the administrator and professional levels served as dependent variables. These models explained about one-third of the variance in the growth rates at those select occupational levels. In basic form they did not differ from the two general models presented in Table 3.

Black Employment, Economic Forces and Public Policy

Analysts must be interested in minority progress in public sector jobs not only because of a concern with fairness and equality values but also for the more prosaic reason that the positions controlled by city hall offer substantial employment opportunities in an uncertain and harsh economy, particularly in deteriorating cities. In 1980 more than 90,000 jobs were held by blacks in the 34 cities in the present sample. Assuming theoretically that one job can support between three and four people, municipal employment could support between 4.5 and 6 percent of the nearly 6 million black residents of the sample cities.

One question that must be asked in this context is whether the local public sector can be made to absorb more of the workers on or outside the margins of the private sector labor market, particularly blacks, whose unemployment rates traditionally run double those of white workers.

To put such a question is to pose a challenge to policymakers. One set of policy options lies in the field of affirmative action. Here emphasis is placed on opening up existing public sector jobs at all levels and in all functions to minority applicants. Affirmative action policies do little to expand the

Table 3

Black Employment Growth: Two Regression Models

	Model I.	Model II.
Dependent variable	change in percent, black total workforce 1973-1980 $R^2 = .23$	change in fair share, total workforce 1973-1980 $R^2 = .46$
Independent variables:	Beta	Beta
population change, 1970-1980	.120	.881
black population change, 1970-1980	.055	-.548*
growth in per capita local revenues, 1973-1980	.333	.436*
growth of manufacturing jobs, 1972-1977	-.225	-.030
unemployment average, 1975-1979	.441	.451
unemployment change, 1977-1979	.328	.300
growth of federal per capita aid, 1973-1980	-.233	-.631*
growth of federal dependence, 1973-1980	-.051	.284

* p .05
** p .01

public sector workforce. To do this, cities must seek to strengthen and then tap their revenue base.

We have argued in this paper that certain economic forces or transformations affect the local economic base from which cities draw resources to finance their public workforce. Expansion of the economic base should help minority job seekers, while contraction or deterioration should hurt them. Are there economic policy initiatives open to government that will have the effect of expanding minority public employment?

The answer must be a qualified no. Federal aid, we must recall, may increase local revenues but it does not appear to increase black employment. In fact growth of federal assistance is generally negatively related to black employment growth.

The most important factor in explaining expanding black job opportunities is population growth. So far in the United States, no widespread consensus exists to support national policies designed to encourage growth or impede population loss. Local policy efforts to encourage growth through economic development incentives are of dubious efficacy. Population growth and decline seem at the moment more or less beyond the effective reach of conscious policy.

Government may also attack local unemployment through job training and job creation incentives in the hopes of strengthening the municipal tax base, but there is no evidence in our data that reduction of unemployment would lead to more minority jobs in the public sector.

One economic factor positively associated with black employment progress that is open to policy manipulations is growth of per capita local revenues. Such growth is related to increases in federal aid ($r = .58$ and $.38$ with per capita and dependency growth, respectively), but as we have seen, federal aid growth does not increase black employment. Per capita revenue growth is only weakly related to population increases ($r = .08$), growth of manufacturing ($r = .21$), and low average unemployment ($r = .02$). This suggests that revenue growth may instead be more a function of conscious tax policy, specifically of tax effort. By increasing local tax rates municipal governments may not only enlarge or stabilize their workforce but also make possible the expansion of black job opportunities. Increasing local taxes, however, is scarcely a politically realistic or palatable option in most cities these days, particularly those deteriorating ones in the Frostbelt states. We must conclude, then, that conscious initiatives designed to enhance black public employment through efforts to strengthen the local tax base or increase local revenues offer scant promise as methods to increase black municipal employment. Growth and decline of black jobs, all things being equal, are likely to remain subject to natural long-term economic transformations that largely resist government intervention.

FOOTNOTES

[1]A graphic illustration of this phenomenon occurred in Chicago early in 1983, when the city announced a few hundred temporary job openings in its streets department. Thousands of unemployed workers, mostly black, crowded a city park waiting to fill out application forms.

[2]The Houston Police Department, for example, made a much-publicized trip to New York City in the winter of 1982-83 to recruit applicants for its rapidly expanding force.

[3]The Boston Police and Fire Departments were ordered by a Federal District Court in 1982 not to use any layoff system that would reduce the percentage of minorities among the protective forces. The case has been appealed to the Supreme Court.

[4]In several other papers in which I examined cross-sectional relationships I was able to use a larger portion of the sample. See Eisinger (1982a) and (1982b).

[5]The coefficient is significant at the .001 level. City population growth is measured by the percentage change between 1970 and 1980. Only 16 of the 34 cities gained population in the 1970s. Public sector growth is measured by the percentage increase in number of municipal employees between 1973 and 1980. Among the sample cities, 16 saw their workforces actually shrink in this period.

REFERENCES

Advisory Commission on Intergovernmental Relations. 1977. Federal Grants: Their Effect on State-Local Expenditures, Employment Levels, Wage Rates. Washington, D.C.: GPO.

Ashenfelter, O. 1977. "Demand and Supply Functions for State and Local Government Employment: The Effect of Federal Grants on Nonfederal Governmental Wages and Employment." In O. Ashenfelter and W. Oates, eds. Essays in Labor Market Analysis. New York: Halsted: 1-16

Barger, H. 1976. "Images of Bureaucracy: A Tri-Ethnic Consideration." Public Administration Review, 36 (May/June): 287-296.

126 Affirmative Action

Eisinger, P. 1982a "Black Employment in Municipal Jobs: The Impact of Black Political Power." American Political Science Review, 76 (June): 380-392.

____. 1982b "The Economic Conditions of Black Employment in Municipal Bureaucracies." American Journal of Political Science, 26 (November): 754-771.

Frederickson, H. 1967. "Understanding Attitudes Toward Public Employment." Public Administration Review, 27 (December): 411-420

Grosskopf, S. 1981. "Public Employment's Impact on the Future of Urban Economies." In R. Bahl, ed. Urban Government Finance. Beverly Hills, Calif.: Sage: 39-62.

Joint Center for Political Studies. 1982. Blacks on the Move: A Decade of Demographic Change. Washington, D.C.: JCPS.

Levine, C., I. Rubin, and G. Wolohojian. 1981. The Politics of Retrenchment. Beverly Hills, Calif.: Sage:

Lupsha, P. and W. Siembieda. 1977. "The Poverty of Public Services in the Land of Plenty." In D. Perry and A. Watkins, eds. The Rise of the Sunbelt Cities. Beverly Hills, Calif.: Sage: 169-190.

New York City Commission on Human Rights. 1976. City Layoffs: The Effect on Minorities and Women.

Reischauer, R. 1981. "The Economy and the Federal Budget in the 1980s: Implications for the State and Local Sector." In R. Bahl, ed. Urban Government Finance. Beverly Hills, Calif.: Sage: 13-38.

Sawhill, I. 1982. "Economic Policy." In J. Palmer and I. Sawhill, eds. The Reagan Experiment. Washington, D.C.: The Urban Institute: 31-58.

Thomas, J. 1978. "Budget Cutting and Minority Employment in City Governments." The Public Personnel Management, 7 (May/June): 155-161.

U.S. Bureau of the Census. 1980. 1977 Census of Manufacturers. Washington, DC: GPO.

_____. 1982. 1980 Census of Population, Supplementary Report. "Standard Metropolitan Statistical Areas and Standard Consolidated Areas, 1980." Washington, D.C.: GPO.

U.S. Bureau of Labor Statistics (annual) <u>State, County and Selected City Employment and Unemployment.</u> Washington, D.C.: microfiche.

Grace Hall Saltzstein

Affirmative Action, Organizational Constraints, and Employment Change

The involvement of the federal government in provision of equal opportunity has been characterized by gradual expansion of non-discrimination provisions over time, from Roosevelt's 1941 executive order barring discrimination by the federal government and defense contractors, through passage of Title VII of the Civil Rights Act of 1964, to recent amendments regarding sex discrimination on the basis of pregnancy. In this developmental process, females were added to the list of protected groups for the first time in 1964, and in 1972 state and local governments were added to the list of employers prohibited from discriminating against protected groups. While congressional action and innovation in this policy arena may have run its course (Burstein and MacLeod, 1980), developments have continued in regard to judicial interpretation and administrative implementation, and both have been shaped by changes in conceptualization of the causes and nature of barriers to employment opportunity (U.S. Commission on Civil Rights, 1981). Over time, there has been a gradual shift, in law and judicial interpretation, away from requirements for "gender or color-blind" hiring decisions that operate in a purely neutral fashion to affirmative action approaches that seek to redress past injustices (U.S. Equal Employment Opportunity Commission, 1979, Ch. II).

In part, this shift has occurred out of a growing realization that the negative results of discrimination are not the exclusive product of individual acts of discrimination but are the culmination of a complex interaction of individual prejudices, social and institutional inequities, and historical forces (U.S. Commission on Civil Rights, 1981). In particular, concern has focused on presumably neutral institutional mechanisms that

128

seem to disproportionately disadvantage women and minorities in employment matters. Such "institutional discrimination" (Feagin and Feagin, 1978) is now thought to perpetuate inequity even in the absence of overtly discriminatory organizational rules and procedures (such as "male only" want ads or separate lines of seniority). Hence, remedies to eliminate discrimination have come to include compensation to injured individuals or groups and to require removal of any and all ". . . unnecessary barriers to employment when barriers operate invidiously to discriminate on the basis of racial or other impermissible classification" (Griggs v. Duke Power Co., 401 U.S. 424; 1971).

Potential barriers to equal employment opportunity are perhaps nowhere as ubiquitous as they are in state and local governments saddled with personnel systems that are the product of decades of reforms designed to insulate personnel matters from politics. Hence, state and local governments are characterized by varying degrees of adherence to merit system norms that demand recruitment, selection, and advancement based solely on merit. In practice, the desired neutral competence has been sought through reliance on rankings derived from test scores on civil service exams and other "objective" evaluations, and deviation from the goal of hiring the most able has been discouraged by adoption of such certification techniques as the rule of three, or, in some cases, the rule of one. At the same time, such goals have been compromised in numerous state and local governments to provide veterans with employment and/or promotion advantages in reward for military service to the country. All of these policies have been criticized for their potential impact on employment opportunity.

The merit system itself has faced considerable attack for some time for the organizational rigidities that it creates that actually impede attainment of merit (Savas and Ginsburg, 1973). Critics contend that "the excessively rigid procedures for entering and advancing in most merit systems have long been recognized as being hindrances to effective management practices" (Shafritz, 1975: 3). Additionally, critics charge that these rigidities are incompatible with efforts to promote equity in employment opportunity (Kranz, 1974; Nigro, 1974; Backoff and Rainey, 1977). Excessive reliance on credentials, pen and paper tests, and quantified results of interviewer assessments of aptitude or motivation presumably has hindered efforts to hire more minorities and females. Congressional hearings on extension of Title VII to state and local governments through the 1972 amendments noted these specific problems and concluded that, "Many civil service rules and procedures . . . may themselves constitute systemic barriers to minorities and women."[1]

More entrenched merit systems tend also to utilize techniques to "certify" applicants for openings by ranking applicants according to their combined scores on the various components of the exams and then limiting hiring agents' choice to the top three (or sometimes one) individuals on the list. As has been noted eleswhere (Savas and Ginsburg, 1973), substantial numbers of applicants typically score within one or two percentage points of one another,[2] raising serious questions about the feasibility of classifying the top three scorers as the "best" applicants. Yet minorities and women (for different reasons) are rarely among the top three scorers, which makes it difficult to increase their ranks in the workforce.

The specific institutional barriers that limit minority opportunities in public personnel systems seem to differ from those that impede female progress. For minorities, the primary barrier in the civil service system appears to be the testing and certification system (Zashin, 1980). For women, the primary barrier, in conjunction with rules of three or one, seems to be the veterans' preference system. At the federal level (where most evaluations have been performed), women may outscore men on exams but lose out in placement because of a lack of veterans' preference points. A Federal Personnel Management Project taskforce in 1977 noted that a 5-point preference (usually a non-disabled veteran) is equal to two or more years of job-related experience, training, or education on an unwritten exam, or 19% more correct answers on the Junior Federal Assistant Examination (cited in Zashin, 1980, fn. 14). Hence, a Government Accounting Office study concluded that women need considerably higher qualifications to compete with even the five-point veterans (Zashin, 1980). This barrier could be even more serious in state and local government systems in which absolute preference may exist, and has been upheld by the courts (Adams, 1980; Blumberg, 1976-77; Fleming and Shanor, 1977).

Many scholars and activists have come to believe that ". . . the systemic aspects of personnel management — job information networks, position requirements, merit selection procedures, career ladders, lateral transfer provisions, training, veterans' preference — crucially influence the ultimate outcomes, i.e., the sex/race composition of entrants and of the workforce in particular occupational series and grade levels" (Zashin, 1980: 354-355). This awareness has worked its way into planning for affirmative action in public personnel systems. A Policy Statement on Voluntary Affirmative Action for State and Local Governments, issued by the U.S. Equal Employment Opportunity Commission (EEOC), the U.S. Department of Justice, Labor, Treasury, and the U.S. Civil Service Commission in 1976, explicitly reflects such thinking by noting that race, sex, color, or ethnic "conscious" steps may be necessary for public employers to overcome the negative results of current personnel systems and practices. <u>Guidelines on Affirmative Action Appropriate Under Title VII as amended</u> (U.S. EEOC, 1979) reaffirms this view and delineates circumstances that warrant remedial action (such as adoption of goals and timetables). Subsequent standards developed by the Office of Personnel Management (1979) require compliance with the <u>Guidelines,</u> including alteration of existing policies and practices that cannot be shown to be job-related. In moving in the direction of challenging current practices, the Chair of the U.S. Civil Service Commission has noted:

> Affirmative action is not an exception to merit . . . it is wrong to assume that merit principles must be compromised to accomplish affirmative action. What sometimes happens is confusion of the word merit with some of the trappings of merit . . . certain current practices, regulations, and laws, which in fact are not essential to a merit system are sometimes the very ones which simultaneously inhibit the accomplishment of affirmative action goals.[3]

Court interpretations have suggested further that the requirements of Title VII supersede state or local civil service laws, rules or regulations that may be in conflict (U.S. EEOC, 1979).

Attempts to deal with the perceived discriminatory impact of certain civil service regulations have led to a collection of various tools, techniques, and organizational strategems to enhance employment opportunities. The assumptions that underlie such affirmative action (AA) approaches vary considerably, with some strategies based on assumptions that employers' attitudes are most significant. The concern here is with those attempts to mitigate perceived organizational barriers to affirmative action. In that regard, at least three major pressures have come to be associated with state and local government affirmative action:

> (1) Special efforts of analysis, validation, reporting and justification of personnel procedures, aimed at removing obstacles to equal employment opportunity (EEO).

(2)   Pressures for alterations of personnel procedures and structure:
(a)   for lowering or removal of
certain standards, requirements, or practices (such as
certain written tests or high
school diploma requirements)
that are not job-related.
(b)   for alteration of selection
and certification procedures,
and other employment
procedures (sometimes, for
"selective certification," for
"hire, then train" procedures,
for special pre-examination
tutoring, for restructuring of
tasks to allow for upward
mobility), to remove
obstacles to EEO.
(3)   Pressure for numerical
representativeness -- for a degree
of preference for minorities/
females in personnel procedures,
where failure to prefer them
cannot be substantiated on the
basis of clearly valid or job-
related criteria, and where their
presence in the organization is
clearly lower than their presence
in the local population (Backoff
and Rainey, 1977: 126).

Those responsible for or interested in state and local
government affirmative action have debated various reforms to
respond to the above pressures. The first pressure is usually
handled by adoption of an AA plan, though there is disagreement
as to what the plan should include. Response to pressures for
alteration of personnel procedures and structures has led to calls
for removal or alteration of veterans' preference policies,
changes in certification techniques (i.e., adoption of rule of the
list instead of rule of three, or adoption of rule of the list
instead of rule of one, or adoption of selective certification[4]
provisions), or (as noted) provisions for pre-exam tutoring or on-
the-job training. Creation of organizational responses to
maintain pressure for "results" has varied, with debate on this
topic frequently centering upon where organizational
responsibility for EEO/AA should be housed (Hutchison, Walton,
and Brawner, 1974).

With recent retreat from policies of affirmative action, proponents of AA techniques are disadvantaged because of the lack of empirical verification of the utility of affirmative action. The overwhelming problem in evaluating the utility of organizational responses to affirmative action pressures in local governments is simply that next to nothing is known about any given aspect of the problem. Very little is known about 1) current personnel practices and procedures, 2) the actual impact of those procedures on female or minority employment representation, 3) the nature and incidence of organizational responses to AA pressures, or 4) the actual impact of those organizational responses on female or minority employment gains. The availability of data regarding existing personnel procedures and practices is extremely limited. Very little is known about such matters as the proportion merit systems, restrictive vs. non-restrictive certification techniques, or veterans' preference systems,[5] nor is it known if there are any predictable variations in the types of cities having certain policies.

Because of the lack of data, very little is known about how significant a barrier current personnel practices are to minority or female job aspirations. On the one hand, studies of federal-level merit systems and veterans' preference systems suggest that such systems may indeed serve as formidable obstacles to equal employment representation (Zashin, 1980; U.S. General Accounting Office, 1977). On the other hand, scholars have long recognized the extent to which seemingly rigid state and local merit systems have succumbed to the demands of patronage (Tolchin and Tolchin, 1972; Shafritz, 1975; Willbern, 1967), suggesting a degree of permeability that could be utilized to obtain AA goals. Individual case studies of local governments support this notion of potential merit system acquiescence to AA (Eisenger, 1982; Thompson, 1975), and isolated studies further suggests that perceived barriers may not be particularly significant in practice.[6] However, there are yet no systematic, comparative analyses of the relationship between personnel systems and female or minority employment opportunity.

Similarly, while macro-level analyses of the impact of EEO laws on the economic situation of women and minorities abound (i.e., Burstein, 1979; Beller, 1980; McCrone and Hardy, 1978), little is known about the nature and scope of local governments' organizational responses to affirmative action or of the impact of those responses on employment representation of females or minorities. Anecdotal evidence regarding the presumed impact of a specific organizational change is common (i.e., Garnier and Potts, 1975), but, again, systematic analyses examining the relative impacts of personnel policies and changes in those policies on actual representation in local governments are limited in number (Renick, 1981; Sigelman, 1976; Meier, 1978).

The study presented here seeks to fill in some of these gaps in the literature regarding affirmative action, organizational constraints, and female employment representation in municipal governments. Data have been collected for this study from a large number of cities to ascertain the nature of existing personnel policies and veterans' preference policies, the extent to which cities have adopted various affirmative action components, and the relationships among and between these characteristics and actual representation of females in the workforce and change in that representation.

Research Design

The universe of American cities employing between 500 and 10,000 workers, in common functions only, was selected as the sample (N = 268) (U.S. Census of Governments, 1972). The cities were contacted with requests for employment data, to be obtained from EEO-4 reports filed annually with the Federal government, regarding female employment representation in eight common functions at various levels for the years 1975 and 1980. One hundred and seventy-four cities, or 64.9% of the total, ultimately responded with usable data. Questionnaires were subsequently sent to these 174 cities requesting specific information regarding veterans' preference systems, personnel systems, and affirmative action provisions. Responses on this portion of the study were obtained from all 174 cities.

Dependent variables utilized in the analysis represent the female share of total general employment representation in the functions of financial administration, police services, fire services, parks and recreation, streets and highways, sanitation and sewage, utilities and transportation, and community development[7] in 1975 and 1980; and the change in that representation during that period. Independent variables assess the presence or absence of various personnel characteristics, veterans' preference characteristics, and AA as of 1975, and whether any of those systems has been altered (and in what fashion) between 1975 and 1980. Personnel system characteristics include the presence of a Civil Service Commission, full-time personnel officer, central personnel office, merit system, state control of merit system, year of adoption of merit, the extensiveness of merit system coverage in 1975, and the nature of the certification process. Veterans' preference characteristics concern the presence or absence of veterans' preference, the year adopted, the nature of the coverage (bonus points on some, most, or all employment exams,

absolute preference, life-time preference, etc.), and the extent
of state control over the system. Questions pertaining to
affirmative action assessed the presence or absence of an
affirmative action plan, the year of its adoption, characteristics
of the EEO function (separate office, department, full-time
director, etc.), organizational location of the EEO/AA function
(personnel, Civil Service Commission, office of the chief
executive, or part of another department or office), and the
presence or absence of specific provisions designed to upgrade
female or minority employment representation (selective certification, pre-exam tutoring, on-the-job training, replacement of
rule of one or three with rule of ranks or rule of the list).

The first concern of the analysis is with the actual employment representation of women. Table 1 presents summary
statistics on the dependent variables and compares those with
similar figures published by the EEOC from the EEO-4 reports.

Table 1.

Female Employment Status and Change in Status in Municipal
Governments Nationwide, 1975-1980 (N=174)

	1980 Female Representation[a]	1975-80 Change, Representation
Range (minimum-maximum)	6.2%-35.5%	-6.5%-17.8%
Mean	17.6	+2.9
Standard deviation	4.7	3.4
U.S. totals,[b] 1978 X	15.3	
U.S. totals,[b] change X 1975-78		+2.2
Average workforce representation, X 1975	37.4	

[a] Full-time employment only, in eight common functions.

[b] Summary totals for all jurisdictions submitting data to U.S.
Equal Employment Opportunity Commission, for eight
functions only, 1975 and 1978.

Source: EEOC State and Local Government Information (EEO-
4), 1975 and 1980: Reports and/or data from reports
furnished by cities to author.

As noted, the female share of total full-time employment in these functions in 1980 ranges from a low of 6.2% to a high of 35.5%, with an average female representation in these functions of 17.6% (compared to an average workforce representation of 37.4%). These 1980 totals represent an average five-year increase in the female share of total employment of 2.9%. The average representation figures and the change in representation are compatible with EEOC summary data for all municipalities nationwide.[8].

Table 2 details the major features of existing personnel systems and veterans' preference systems in these municipal governments. As is evident, formalized personnel systems are the norm. Most of these cities had central personnel offices and a full-time personnel officer as of 1975, and nearly two-thirds had a Civil Service Commission. Merit systems influence is pervasive, though a total of 46 cities report no merit systems at all. Of those having a merit system, over half extend merit coverage to 90% or more of their employees. Additionally, a clear majority of those having merit systems (70%) have also adopted a rule of three or one in the certification process. Veterans' preference requirements are somewhat less common, but state influence is more pervasive in those that do have systems. Nearly 60% of those that do have veterans' preference requirements are part of a state-wide system of preference; 84% of that group cannot alter the preference requirements without state permission. Most cities that have veterans' preference provisions provide some system of bonus points on employment exams for most or all positions; lifetime preferences are considerably less common; and absolute reference for veterans is found in only seven cities.

There is clearly variation in the incidence and nature of organizational constraints that might serve as barriers to female employment opportunity. Until very recently, considerable pressures have been exerted by the courts and the Federal government for municipalities to alter the nature of these constraints. Table 2 also indicates how cities have organized to respond to these pressures (or in anticipation of these pressures). Most cities now have affirmative action plans, though there is considerable variation as to the year in which such plans were adopted. Most cities (69.7%) lodge responsibility for EEO/AA in the personnel department or the Civil Service Commission, 15% place such responsibility in such non-personnel offices as Community Development or Human Relations, and another 15% house EEO/AA responsibility in the office of the Chief Executive (i.e., mayor or manager). Alternation of existing organizational constraints or adoption of alternative mechanisms to overcome organizational barriers is

Table 2.

Incidence of Personnel, Veterans' Preference,
and Affirmative Action
System Characteristics in 174 Municipal Governments, 1975

Organizational Characteristic or Institutional Mechanism	Number of Cities (Percent of total cities)
Personnel Characteristics:	
Civil Service Commission	114 (65.5)
Central personnel office	149 (85.6)
Presence of merit system	125 (71.8)
State-wide merit system	34 (19.5)
Certification process:	
No process	27 (15.5)
Rule of 5 or 7	13 (7.5)
Rule of 3	76 (43.7)
Rule of 1	11 (6.3)
Veterans' Preference Characteristics:	
Veterans' preference	107 (62.6)
State-wide system	62 (35.6)
Bonus points only on most employment exams	74 (42.5)
Absolute preference	7 (4.0)
Life-time preference	30 (17.2)
Affirmative Action Characteristics:	
Adoption of AA plan	160 (92)
Organizational location of EEO/AA responsibilities:	
Personnel Dept. or CSC	115 (69.7)
Human Relations Office, Dept. of Human Rights, etc.	25 (15.0)
Office of Chief Executive (mayor, city manager, etc.)	25 (15.0)
Provision for:	
Selective certification	22 (14.7)
Pre-exam tutoring	40 (22.9)
On-the-job training	13 (7.4)
Changing from more restrictive certification system to rule of ranks or rule of the list	44 (24)

SOURCE: Questionnaires completed by cities and furnished to author

not widespread in these cities at this time. Adoption of pre-exam tutoring and a rule of ranks or rule of the list for selection are the most popular, but have been adopted in less than 25% of the cities. Only 14% of the cities have adopted provisions for selective certification of applicants, and less than 8% provide on-the-job training as part of their EEO efforts.

Correlates of Employment Representation

Regression analysis is utilized to assess the relative effects of affirmative action systems, personnel system characteristics, and veterans' preference systems on overall female employment representation and changes in representation from 1975 to 1980. The results of the analysis are presented in Table 3. A number of points stand out. First, it is clear that these institutional constraints or opportunities can account for only limited amounts of the variation in either overall female employment representation or changes in such representation. Numerous studies suggest that female employment representation in any given arena is the consequence of a complex array of personal, institutional, and systemwide choices, and any subset of that array of female representation.

However, the relationships evident here are clear, consistent, and follow expected patterns. The relative strengths of the various factors are also notable. It appears that operating under a state-wide merit system, utilizing a rule of three in the hiring process, and employing some system of veterans' preference all have a negative effect on total female employment representation and changes in representation. On the other hand, the presence of a central personnel office (indicative of a more bureaucratized organization) is associated with higher levels of representation, accounting for ten percent of the variation in overall female representation.

Housing EEO/AA responsibilities in the office of the Chief Executive is the only affirmative action characteristic that proves to be related to overall female representation and changes in representation. Indeed, even after controlling for all other variables, this factor is the most significant correlate of female representation, accounting for nine percent of total representation and eight percent of the change in representation. Those cities which housed responsibility for the EEO/AA function in the Chief Executive's office as of 1975 had a mean representation of females in 1980 of 20.8% and had increased such representation an average of 5.2% during the period 1975-1980. This is contrasted with a 1980 mean representation level of 17% and a mean change of 2.6% in those cities which house EEO/AA someplace other than the Chief Executive's office.

At least one possible explanation for the significance of the organizational location of EEO/AA responsibilities is immediately evident. Thus, housing EEO/AA in the office of the Chief Executive might reflect organizational commitment to the program. Others have conceptualized organizational commitment to AA in a narrower, bureaucratic sense (see Bellone and Darling, 1980; Renick, 1981) and hence have overlooked the more "political" implications of organizational location. It is possible that placing EEO/AA responsibilities in a highly visible location, under the apparent protection of the Chief Executive, provides an AA office with the clout that is needed to produce results.

Table 3.
Effect of Systemic Barriers and Affirmative
Action on Female Employment

	1980 Female Employment Representation		Change in Employment Representation 1975-80	
	Beta	R^2 Change	Beta	R^2 Change
Civil Service Commission	.04	.00	.00	.00
Central personnel office	.25**	.10	.10	.01
State-wide merit system	-.18**	.04	-.13**	.03
Year adopted merit system	-.05*	.01	-.09	.01
Rule of three	-.11*	.01	-.17**	.05
Veterans' preference	-.15**	.03	-.12**	.02
Bonus points for veterans on employment exams	-.07	.00	.01	.00
Year adopted Affirmative Action Plan	-.07	.00	-.03	.00
EEO/AA housed in office of Chief Executive	.30**	.09	.29**	.08
	R^2 = .27		R^2 = .20	

*Significant at .05 level of confidence
**Significant at .01 level of confidence

Conclusions

This analysis provides a basis for some conclusions regarding organizational barriers to employment opportunities for females in municipal government employment and the impact of affirmative action in the municipal government setting. First, it should be reiterated that institutional obstacles in the aggregate do not appear to be the major causes or predictors of female employment representation or change in that representation.[9] Though the impacts are all in the expected directions, taken together, institutional barriers explain barely 8% of the variation in female employment representation in 1980 and little more than 10% of the change in representation over time. Further, countervailing pressures that are associated with female employment gains are evident in some cities and may serve to mitigate the deleterious effects of systemic barriers.

Whatever the combined effects of institutional barriers might be in municipal governments, this analysis suggests that organizational commitment to affirmative action may overcome such barriers so as to enhance female job opportunities. In this setting, organizational commitment seems to be best expressed by early adoption of an AA plan and assignment of EEO/AA responsibility to the Chief Executive's office. Again, what this reinforces is that perspective that sees organizational decision-rules as being permeable to external forces. Municipal personnel systems have bent to accommodate patronage appointments for decades; now perhaps they are giving way to demands for increased representation of females and minorities. Further, some change apparently can be accomplished without any alteration of existing personnel constraints.

The affirmative action factor that is associated with positive change is simply that of organizational location of the EEO/AA responsibility. Such a finding is wholly in keeping with analyses of the politics of organization. As Seidman (1970, p. 14 notes):

> Organizational arrangements are not neutral. We do not organize in a vacuum. Organization is one way of expressing . . . commitment, influencing program direction, to give some interests, some perspectives, more access to those with decision-making authority.

Locating AA responsibilities in the office of the Chief Executive is suggestive of exceptive concern with and interest in AA and is related to AA results. Further research is needed to determine the circumstances which lead to this organizational arrangement. What cities adopt such an arrangement and why? Some analyses of the political and environmental factors that are associated with this organizational arrangement are needed to provide a basis for disentangling the relative influences of organization and environment on outcomes and determining the independent effects of organizational location on AA results.

FOOTNOTES

[1]Legislative History of the Equal Employment Opportunity Act of 1972, p. 423, cited in EEOC (1979, p. II-4). This legislative overview is drawn to a large extent from that analysis.

[2]Savas and Ginsberg (1973) point to a 1968 exam for Fire Lieutenant in New York City, on which 25 men scored between 86 and 87, and 203 scored between 81 and 82.

[3]Campbell, cited in EEOC (1979, p. III-4). See also D. Stewart (1980) for an analysis of this changing view of merit.

[4]Selective certification provisions typically allow for addition of qualified applicants from specific underrepresented groups to the register from which final selections are made.

[5]This data gap has long been recognized, and sporadic attempts have been made to fill the gap (e.g., Harrison, 1971; Saso and Tanis, 1974), but little data are collected on a regular basis and data in certain areas (local government veterans' preference) are virtually non-existent.

[6]The City of Berkeley, California, for example, conducted a study of actual use of veterans' preference points in City employment and found that the number of individuals appointed with points was so small that the system could hardly be considered a major barrier to EEO.

[7]These represent the major functions that are common to most cities in the sample.

[8]National summaries are not available in comparable form for the years 1979 and 1980. National figures listed in Table 1 have been computed only for the eight common functions used in this analysis. The national figures listed are, therefore, lower than those reported by Cayer and Sigelman (1980) because Table 1 figures do not include such female-dominated functions as health and hospitals (which are not common to all cities).

[9]This macro-level conclusion does not, of course, provide justification for continuation of such policies if they have an adverse impact on individual applicants and cannot be shown to be job-related.

REFERENCES

Adams, C. 1980. "Constitutional Law: Veterans' Preference Statute Survives Gender-Based Equal Protection Challenge." Washburn Law Journal, 19: pp. 365-373.

Backoff, R. W. and H. G. Rainey. 1977. "Technology, Professionalization, Affirmative Action, and the Merit System." C. H. Levine, ed. (1977), Managing Human Resources, Volume 13, Urban Affairs Annual Reviews (Beverly Hills: Sage Publishers).

Beller, A. H. 1980. "The Effect of Economic Conditions on the Success of Equal Employment Opportunity Laws: An Application to the Sex Differential in Earnings" Review of Economics and Statistics, 62, 3: pp. 379-387.

Bellone, C. H. and D. H. Darling. 1980. "Implementing Affirmative Action Programs: Problems and Strategies." Public Personnel Management, 9, 3: pp. 184-191.

Blumberg, G. 1976-77. "De Facto and De Jure Sex Discrimination Under the Equal Protection Clause: A Reconsideration of the Veterans' Preference in Public Employment." Buffalo Law Review, 26 (Fall/Winter): pp. 3-82.

Burstein, P. 1979. "Equal Employment Opportunity Legislation and the Income of Women and Nonwhites," American Sociological Review, 44 (June): pp. 367-391.

Burstein, P. and M. W. MacLeod. 1980. "Prohibiting Employment Discrimination: Ideas and Politics in the Congressional Debate over Equal Employment Opportunity Legislation." American Journal of Sociology, 86, 3, 512-533.

Cayer, N. J. and L. Sigelman. 1980. "Minorities and Women in State and Local Government: 1973-75." Public Administration Review, 40 (Sept./Oct.): pp. 443-451.

Eisinger, P. 1982. "Black Employment in Municipal Jobs: The Impact of Political Power." The American Political Science Review, 76 (June): pp. 380-392.

Feagin, J. and C. B. Feagin. 1978. Discrimination American Style (Englewood Cliffs, N.J.: Prentice-Hall, Inc.).

Fleming, J. H. and C. A. Shanor. 1977. "Veterans' Preferences in Public Employment: Unconstitutional Gender Discrimination?" Emory Law Journal, 26: pp. 13-64.

Garnier, R. and D. Potts. 1975. "Selective Certification for Affirmative Action." Personnel Letter (International Personnel Management Association, March 1975), pp. 3-5.

Harrison, B. 1971. "State and Local Government Manpower Policies." Industrial Relations, 10, 1:

Hutchison, R. W., E. Walton, and J. Brawner. 1974. "The Organization of Affirmative Action in 49 U.S. Federal Agencies." Public Personnel Management (July/August): pp. 289-294.

Kranz, H. 1974. "Are Merit and Equity Compatible?" Public Administration Review, 34 (Sept./Oct.): 434-44.

McCrone, D. and R. Hardy. 1978. "Civil Rights Policies and the Achievement of Racial Economic Equality, 1948-1975." American Journal of Political Science, 22: pp. 1-17.

Meier, K. 1978. "Constraints on Affirmative Action." Policy Studies Journal, 7 (Winter): pp. 208-212.

Nigro, L. G., ed. 1974. "Minisymposium on Affirmative Action in Public Administration." Public Administration Review, 34 (May/June): 234-246.

Renick, J. C. 1981. "The Impact of Municipal Affirmative Action Programs on Black Representation in Government Employment: Reality or Rhetoric?" Southern Review of Public Administration, Summer: pp. 127-146.

Saso, C. D. and E. P. Tanis. 1974. Selection and Certification of Eligibles. Personnel Report No. 743 (Chicago, Ill.: International Personnel Management Association).

Savas, E. S. and S. G. Ginsburg (1973). "The Civil Service: A Meritless System." The Public Interest, 32, pp. 72-85.

Seidman, H. 1970. Politics, Position and Power: The Dynamics of Federal Organization (New York: Oxford University Press).

Shafritz, J. M. 1975. Public Personnel Management: The Heritage of Civil Service Reform (New York: Praeger Publishers).

Sigelman, L. 1976. "The Curious Case of Women in State and Local Governments." Social Science Quarterly, 56 (March): pp. 591-604.

Stewart, D. 1980. "Merit Systems in the 1980's." Public Personnel Management: Problems and Prospects. S. Hays and D. Kearney, eds. (1980).

144   Affirmative Action

Thompson, F. 1975. Personnel Policy in the City (Berkeley: University of California Press).

Tolchin, M. and S. Tolchin. 1971. To the Victor -- Political Patronage from the Clubhouse to the White House New York: Random House.

U.S. Commission on Civil Rights. 1981. Affirmative Action in the 1980 s: Dismantling the Process of Discrimination (Washington, D.C.: U.S. Government Printing Office).

U.S. Equal Employment Opportunity Commission. 1979. Eliminating Discrimination in Employment: A Compelling National Priority (Washington, D.C.: U.S. Government Printing Office).

U.S. Equal Employment Opportunity Coordinating Council. 1976. A Policy Statement on Voluntary Affirmative Action for State and Local Governments, 41 FR 38814 (Sept. 13, 1976).

U.S. Equal Employment Opportunity Commission. 1979. Guidelines on Affirmative Action Appropriate under Title VII, as amended, 44 FR 4422 (Jan. 19, 1979).

U.S. Government Accounting Office. 1977. Conflicting Congressional Policies: Veterans' Preference and Appointment vs. Equal Employment Opportunity (Washington, D.C.: U.S. GAO).

U.S. Office of Personnel Management. 1979. Standards for a Merit System of Personnel Administration, 5 CFR 900.601 (h) 44 FR 10238 (Feb. 16, 1979).

Willbern, Y. 1967. "Personnel and Money," The 50 States and Their Local Governments. J. W. Fesler, ed., (New York: Knopf).

Zashin, E. M. 1980. "Affirmative Action and Federal Personnel Systems." Public Poli~, 2, 3: 351-380.

Part IV
The Future of Affirmative Action

Jeremy Plant
Frank J. Thompson

Deregulation, the Bureaucracy, and Employment Discrimination: The Case of the EEOC

The Equal Employment Opportunity Commission (EEOC) ranks among the major regulatory bureaucracies of the federal government. As the curtain rose on the 1980s, the agency assumed center stage in the federal government's campaign against employment discrimination. President Carter's Reorganization Plan Number 1 of 1978 had bolstered the EEOC's authority substantially. It expanded the protected classes that fell within the agency's bailiwick from the groups covered under Title VII of the Civil Rights Act (those based on "race, color, religion, sex or national origin") to the elderly and certain of the handicapped (those working for the federal government). It expanded the EEOC's jurisdiction to cope with a particular kind of discrimination--that covered by the Equal Pay Act. It added the federal government to the cluster of employers subject to the agency's regulation. By the end of the 1970s, the EEOC's jurisdiction extended to 70 percent of some 100 million members of the civilian work force (General Accounting Office, 1981: 5). While supporting actors, such as the Department of Labor, continued to play pertinent roles in the equal employment drama, the EEOC appeared on the top line of the marquee.

The late 1970s and early 1980s also witnessed another important development for equal employment opportunity--the growth of pressure for deregulation. Since personnel systems allocate such scarce values as material perquisites, power, authority, and psychic gratification to various groups in society, any movement toward the deregulation of these systems warrants careful attention. By analyzing the case of the EEOC, this essay strives to enhance understanding of regulatory bureaucracies and their susceptibility to White House pressures for deregulation. In this regard, deregulation via the bureaucracy and implementation process comprises the primary focus (Thompson, 1982: 202-212). In a nutshell, what can the institutions of the presidency do to spawn deregulation without fundamental modifications in the statutes that govern the agency?

The essay begins by examining potential paths to deregulation at the EEOC and explains the rationale for focusing on enforcement rather than rule revocation. It then assesses the utility of four resources that the White House could use in an effort to galvanize enforcement deregulation--presidential status, appointment authority, prosecutorial dependence and budget control. The essay shows that the effective use of any of these resources is greatly complicated by a major characteristic of the EEOC's technology, namely, the coproduction of inspections and prosecutorial sanctions. A final section examines the more general implications of the agency's experience for the politics of deregulation and compliance.

In attempting to fathom the dynamics of deregulation, this essay draws on diverse sources of information--in depth open-ended interviews with key actors, public documents, the media, and scholarly literature. While these methods do not permit the rigorous testing of hypotheses, they can facilitate the generation of propositions. Given current levels of understanding about the nature and causes of deregulation via the bureaucracy, exploratory studies can legitimately claim a place on the research agendas of social scientists (Yin, 1982: 36-72).

ENFORCEMENT DEREGULATION AS A FOCUS

Regulation is a process involving the intentional restriction of some targeted group's choice alternatives by a government agency through the promulgation of directives, or rules, and the threat of penalties for failure to comply with them. Given this definition, deregulation can assume two major forms. First, standards, or rules, deregulation occurs when formal requirements or guidelines promulgated by the agency demand less of the target group or when increasing numbers of this group are exempted from the rules entirely. The EEOC could, for instance, lessen the reporting requirements for employers or cease to require certain of them to fill out forms at all. Second, enforcement deregulation sets in when shrinkage occurs in the agency's capacity or will to detect violations of standards, to cite these infractions, to penalize the target group, and to specify and enforce stringent remedies.

For students of deregulation via the bureaucracy, enforcement rather than standards reduction comprises a more inviting focus in the case of EEOC. This is primarily because formal statutory interpretation of employment law tends to be

dominated more by the courts than the bureaucracy. Many of
the regulatory agencies created during the 1960s and 1970s,
especially those concerned with environmental hazards, played a
lead role in interpreting the law by promulgating a large number
of rules in the Federal Register. In dealing with these agencies,
the courts have typically assumed a highly reactive posture.
They sporadically respond to a plaintiff by either affirming or
infirming a standard issued by the regulatory agency (e.g., with
respect to permissible levels of exposure to some toxic
substance). By contrast, the EEOC has taken a back seat to the
courts in major statutory interpretations. The EEOC
promulgated relatively few formal rules during the 1970s. Only
with the coming of the Carter administration did the pace of
issuing standards quicken appreciably. In 1978, for instance, the
agency set forth uniform guidelines on employee selection that
helped clarify burden-of-proof considerations for those charged
with discrimination. The Carter years also saw guidelines
published on such issues as sexual harassment and age
discrimination. Even then, the practice of issuing these
standards as "guidelines" undercut their force as directives. In
the meantime, the courts have taken the lead in articulating the
standards embedded in Title VII. The Supreme Court in Griggs
vs. Duke Power Company, for instance, did more to define
institutional discrimination and shift the burden of proof to
those accused of violations of Title VII than any rule issued by
the EEOC.

This is not to suggest that a president committed to
deregulation will ignore the administrative rule-making process
at the EEOC. In August, 1981, for instance, the Vice President's
Task Force on Regulatory Relief listed existing regulations that
would be reviewed with an eye toward revising or revoking
them. The list contained two EEOC guidelines--one focused on
sexual harassment and the other on employee selection
procedures. By mid-1984, however, no major rule revocation
had surfaced in the Federal Register.

For those bent on deregulation, a focus on enforcement
rather than standards has several virtues. Rule reduction tends
to be highly visible. Notices frequently need to be published in
the Federal Register and various groups have the opportunity to
comment and appeal. Enforcement deregulation, by contrast,
tends to be more covert and thereby spark less controversy and
resistance. Rule reduction is also expensive. Much staff time
needs to be devoted to documenting the need for weakening
standards. In contrast, enforcement reduction tends to be
perfectly consistent with allocating less money to the agency.

Enforcement reduction at the EEOC could follow several
paths. The atrophy of organizational intelligence comprises a
major one. Such atrophy in part surfaces when a regulatory

agency becomes less knowledgeable about the location and magnitude of violations in its environment. At the EEOC, a degree of atrophy could take hold if individuals subject to discrimination become less willing to file complaints. An accompanying form of intelligence reduction can arise if the agency loses its capacity to investigate complaints and determine their validity. Or the atrophy of intelligence can emerge because of a reduced capacity to obtain a broad overview of patterns of discrimination. Such an overview is essential if the EEOC is to target its litigation efforts effectively.

Movement toward epistemological stringency is another route to enforcement deregulation. The personnel of regulatory agencies must constantly make decisions about what constitutes adequate proof of some empirical claim, e.g., that discrimination exists. These personnel can obviously be more or less stringent in this regard. To the extent that the EEOC demands more proof to conclude that discrimination has occurred, enforcement reduction may well emerge.

Enforcement deregulation can, of course, also surface if the agency obtains less in the way of penalties and corrective actions from those found guilty of discrimination. The agency might, for instance, refrain from pursuing class action suits involving targets and timetables for hiring minorities. Or this type of enforcement reduction could occur in less visible ways. In using the "informal methods of conference, conciliation, and persuasion" emphasized by Title VII, agency personnel might put new pressure on complainants to accept more modest settlements prior to litigation.

While other modes of deregulation could be cited, it should be evident that it is a multidimensional phenomenon. An observer must guard against drawing too many inferences from a stream of events along any one dimension; this stream might be offset elsewhere by developments flowing in quite the opposite direction. With enhanced appreciation of the many faces of deregulation, this essay can turn to the particular issues confronted by a White House inclined toward enforcement reduction via the bureaucracy.

LEVERS OF ENFORCEMENT DEREGULATION

How easy is it for the White House to instigate enforcement reduction at the EEOC? On balance, the evidence suggests that the available levers for such deregulation may work but are likely to be clumsy. In part, the clumsiness of these mechanisms stems from the added measure of authoritative autonomy granted to the agency by its "independent" commission. Unlike many programs of the "new social regulation" that got housed in the line agencies of the federal government, the EEOC represented the old tradition of formal leadership by a commission of five members. The President appoints commissioners with the advice and consent of the Senate for a term of five years and no more than three can be members of the same political party. In making these appointments, the President designates a Chair who assumes responsibility for the "administrative operations" of the agency. The statute broadly empowers the commission "to prevent any person from engaging in any unlawful employment practices." Beyond this, the President possesses the authority to appoint the agency's General Counsel to a four year term with the advice and consent of the Senate. Title VII authorizes the General Counsel to conduct the litigation of the agency and "to assume such other duties as the commission may prescribe."

The presence of a commission need not, of course, effectively buffer the EEOC's core technology from a White House pursuing deregulation. In this regard, Moe has aptly observed that regulatory commissions are "not truly independent of presidential direction and control" (Moe, 1982: 197). He points to four resources in particular that the White House can exploit: presidential status, personnel appointments, prosecutorial dependence, and the budget process.

Presidential Status

Moe argues that one mechanism of presidential influence over commissions stems from the status, or prestige, of the office. In his terms, "many individuals within the commissions may give great weight to the president's policy positions not because he wields rewards and sanctions, but simply because he holds the office of president and, in their minds, has a right to expect compliance" (Moe, 1982: 201). The value of this resource at the EEOC seems minimal, however. Other things being equal, the more that a regulatory agency takes on the attributes of a full-fledged representative bureaucracy the less useful this resource becomes in fostering enforcement deregulation.

A regulatory agency takes on the character of a representative bureaucracy to the degree, first, that its personnel and political audience view it as an advocate for a specific segment of the public. Second, the agency becomes more representative to the degree that it employs members of the group whose interests it seeks to represent. Born in the wake of the civil rights movement, the major internal and external constituencies of the EEOC see it as a leading advocate for minorities, women, and other disadvantaged groups in the labor market. Moreover, at least one of the groups being represented, racial minorities, holds a large proportion of positions in the agency. As of late 1980, for instance, minorities comprised 62 percent of the employees at the EEOC (48 percent were black and 12 percent Hispanic). Furthermore, this demographic pattern prevailed at both the top and bottom levels of the bureaucracy. A majority of the EEOC's employees in the Senior Executive Service as well as Grades 13 through 15 were minority (EEOC, 1981: 26-28).

Some evidence suggests that full-fledged representative bureaucracies working for civil rights disproportionately attract personnel interested in program goals rather than in more narrow personal employment objectives such as promotional opportunities. Racial minorities working in these agencies appear to sustain their commitment to civil rights goals and identify more with minorities in society than white employees (Romzek and Hendricks, 1982: 75-82). Thus, the staff of the EEOC seems unlikely to accord great deference to presidential views if the White House pursues activities that run counter to the vigorous enforcement of civil rights laws.

Perils and Potential of Personnel Appointments

Moe also notes that presidents often have more discretion to appoint the top level personnel of an "independent agency" than at first meets the eye. Chairs of commissions have, for instance, frequently resigned when a new President takes office. The chance to appoint other commissioners may also rapidly emerge. President Reagan, for instance, quickly had the opportunity to replace a majority of the commissioners, including the Chair, as well as the General Counsel.

Appointment authority, however, need not lead to the recruitment of people who share the President's views and who possess the commitment and skills needed to move the agency toward deregulation. Moe himself notes that "rather than moving systematically to maximize his influence over the commissions, the President often uses them as political dumping grounds. . ." (Moe, 1981: 134-137). Even when the White House more conscientiously attempts to shape an agency ideologically, recruitment networks for political executives may thwart him. As another analyst has observed, "Fragmentary national party organizations in the United States have always been an uncertain source of political manpower for managing the executive branch. In recent years, as the demand for more high-caliber political executives has increased, the capacity of established political networks to provide them has declined even further" (Heclo, 1977: 94).

Aside from these complicating factors, the case of the EEOC points to other considerations summed up in the following proposition: Other things being equal, the utility of personnel appointments to accomplish fine - tuned enforcement deregulation decreases to the extent that the regulatory agency is a representative bureaucracy that speaks for a group conspicuously absent from the President's electoral coalition. But while personnel appointments are not a precisely calibrated lever for deregulation, conflict and delay over them can in a less controlled way fuel enforcement reduction.

In considering the plausibility of this proposition, the experience of the Reagan Administration warrants scrutiny. The status of the EEOC as a representative bureaucracy put the Reagan Administration under strong pressure to appoint a minority to chair the commission. Few minority leaders had, however, supported Reagan. Consequently, the President's usual recruitment difficulties became compounded. After considerable delay, Reagan nominated a black businessman named William M. Bell for the position. Bell seemed ideologically compatible with the White House. For instance, he expressed reservations about the use of quotas and timetables for hiring minorities at one point, telling a Senate Committee that "Equality of condition imposed by government is the very definition of tyranny." (Senate Com. on Labor and Human Resources, 1982: 16.) Bell's qualifications seemed so meager, however, that he soon ran into opposition in the Senate. Critics noted that he had never managed more than four employees and that his job placement firm, Bold Concepts, Inc., had not found anyone employment in 1980. The white and yellow pages of the Detroit telephone directory did not even list the firm. Moreover, in an agency where attorneys rank as the dominant professional group, Bell was not a lawyer.

Opposition to Bell became so intense that the President withdrew the nomination in 1982. Soon thereafter, Reagan nominated Clarence Thomas, his Assistant Secretary for Civil Rights in the Department of Education, for the job. Thomas, a black attorney with a degree from Yale Law School, suffered from none of the easy challenges to his qualifications. He skillfully negotiated his way through Senate hearings, hedging on the use of quotas and timetables and skirting persistent inquiries from Senator Eagleton as to whether his philosophy most closely tracked with Ayn Rand, Thomas Sowell or Martin Luther King, Jr. (Senate Com. on Labor and Human Resources, 1982: 16). The Senate rapidly approved the appointment.

The appointment of the General Counsel at the EEOC tends to carry less symbolic baggage. In part because of this, Reagan succeeded in winning rapid approval of Michael J. Connolly, a white lawyer previously employed by General Motors who had considerable experience in the equal employment area. Successful appointment, however, does not assure survival, especially in a representative bureaucracy. Connolly soon came under intense criticism for his views that the EEOC should narrow the scope of sexual harassment cases, discourage age discrimination law-suits, de-emphasize class action

litigation and halt comparable worth investigations. The attack
intensified when he attempted to juggle his staff of senior
attorneys (six of whom were black) without informing the chairman of the commission. The escalating criticism resulted in his
resignation in August, 1982, less than a year after he took
office.

On the surface, then, the experience of the Reagan
Administration bodes poorly for the use of personnel appointments to foster enforcement deregulation. To the extent that
an administration seeks to use these appointments to control the
precise shape of enforcement deregulation, this observation is
sound. However, considerable, if less controlled, enforcement
deregulation may result from turmoil and delay in the personnel
process. A White House can win by disrupting the personnel
game as well as by winning it. At one point, for instance, the
EEOC could not process any litigation for 107 days because the
White House had not appointed enough commissioners to comprise the quorum needed for a vote. Vacancies in and conflict
over the General Counsel position can also inhibit the investigation and filing of suits. While the lower echelons of the EEOC
can continue to process and settle large numbers of claims,
constant tumult over personnel issues at the top of the
organization can take its toll. Career employees in the
organization may feel increasingly frustrated and impotent;
consequently their involvement with and commitment to the
agency may diminish (Romzek and Hendricks, 1982: 75-82).

Prosecutorial Dependence

Moe's analysis also suggests that prosecutorial dependence
on a line agency of the federal government can prompt enforcement deregulation. In general, the greater a regulatory commission's dependence on such an agency to pursue sanctions, the
easier for the White House to foster enforcement deregulation.

Early in its life, the EEOC had to refer suits to the
Department of Justice. In the wake of 1972 revisions in Title
VII, however, the EEOC gained the right to sue directly in the
case of the private sector (employers with 15 or more
employees, employment agencies, labor unions). However, the
law continued to require the EEOC to refer suits against state
and local agencies to the Justice Department. In general, this
department has proven to be more selective than regulatory
agencies in taking cases to court and has typically been willing
to settle for lower penalties (Diver, 1980: 287-288). More
relevant here, the White House has access to enough levers at
Justice to shape the agency's behavior in dealing with equal
employment litigation.

For instance, the Reagan Administration succeeded in
appointing William Bradford Reynolds as Assistant Attorney

General for Civil Rights despite his lack of experience in the area. Subsequent appointments to the Civil Rights Division of Justice also failed to include anyone with a civil rights background. Nor does it appear that racial minorities were appointed to positions of authority (Washington Council of Lawyers, 1983). While the precise pattern of enforcement deregulation under Reynolds awaits subsequent analysis, the Justice Department has clearly abandoned the quest for one of the more stringent remedies in the equal employment arena--targets and timetables for hiring minorities. In 1982, for instance, the Justice Department filed an amicus curiae brief on the side of white police and fire fighters in Boston. These workers had appealed a federal court ruling that ordered the city to lay off white personnel rather than less senior minority workers in order to sustain a proper racial balance. Then, too, in early January, 1983, the Justice Department initiated actions aimed at overturning a judicially imposed agreement under which the City of New Orleans promised to promote equal numbers of black and white officers.

Budget Squeeze

Among the resources a President can use to shape the behavior of regulatory commissions, Moe contends that the Office of Management and Budget is "the most important by far" (Moe, 1982: 201). For those in quest of enforcement deregulation, a budget squeeze tends to rank as the most feasible strategy in dealing with independent agencies that are representative bureaucracies. A budget squeeze can arise from outright cuts in agency resources or the failure of these resources to keep pace with increased demand for services. While defenders of the agency resist a budget squeeze, the symbolism attached to it tends to be less than when the White House uses other deregulation levers. For example, the appointment of executives to the EEOC who lack sympathy for its mission can less readily be construed as anything other than White House hostility. A budget squeeze, by contrast, can parade under the banner of economy and efficiency. Furthermore, the budget process has become increasingly prolonged and complex so that rallying opponents to fight cuts at any one decision point is more difficult.

A budget squeeze tends, of course, to be a blunt instrument of enforcement deregulation. If public officials at times throw money at a problem, they also throw cuts. In theory, of course, agency personnel might respond by getting as much or more enforcement bang for fewer bucks. But the disruptive and demoralizing influences of a budget squeeze may well make the agency less efficient than before. As will become evident in the next section, certain characteristics of the EEOC make this latter development quite likely.

The activities of the Reagan Administration will ultimately provide analysts with case material to examine some of the ramifications of a budget squeeze. Reagan succeeded in applying the brakes to EEOC growth as Table 1 illustrates.

TABLE 1

EEOC APPROPRIATIONS AND PERMANENT
POSITIONS, FISCAL YEARS 1970 - 1984

Fiscal Year	Appropriation (Thousands)	Number of Permanent Positions
1970	$ 13,247	780
1973	31,758	1909
1978	84,550	2837
1979	111,417	3627
1980	124,562	3433
1981	141,200	3412
1982	144,739	3137
1983	147,421	3127
1984	154,039 (estimate)	3127 (estimate)

Sources: Appendix, The Budget of the United States Government, Fiscal Year 1972, 1975, 1980, 1981, 1982, 1983,
1984, 1985 (Washington: U.S. Government Printing
Office).

From fiscal 1970 through 1980, the agency's appropriations grew by 840 percent and its allotment of permanent positions by 340 percent. The early 1980s, by contrast, featured stagnant appropriations and a decline in the number of positions allocated to the agency.

COPRODUCTION AND ENFORCEMENT DEREGULATION

Personnel turmoil, prosecutorial dependence, and budget control do not permit the President to steer deregulation along clearly prescribed paths; but they at least give him a chance to ignite movement in the general direction of enforcement reduction. The dynamics of using these levers as well as their potential for paradox cannot be grasped, however, without examining the critical role of coproduction at the EEOC. More than any other single factor, coproduction increases the burden of calculation for a White House bent on deregulation.

Coproduction refers to involvement by the formally stated beneficiaries of a program in its implementation (Whitaker, 1980: 240-246). Although not on its paid staff, beneficiaries may spend time and energy cooperating with the agency as it attempts to serve their needs. In essence, they become a free resource often allowing the agency to achieve more than it could were it dependent purely on its own resources.

Coproduction in a regulatory agency can assume many guises. Two in particular stand out in the case of the EEOC. One dimension of coproduction involves the degree to which an agency depends on complaints from beneficiaries to shape its allocation of investigatory resources and prosecutorial sanctions. In a sense, beneficiaries might be seen as untrained inspectors who alert the agency to potential violations. In contrast, some regulatory agencies rely on a more proactive approach whereby employees of the agency systematically gather information about violations and then determine who should be prosecuted.

Another dimension of regulatory coproduction involves the extent to which beneficiaries can independently activate the same mechanisms of prosecution that agency personnel use to impose penalties and remedies. In the case of the EEOC, for instance, complainants can sue in federal district court if the agency fails to bring litigation or otherwise achieve settlement within a certain time frame, usually 180 days from the filing of the charge. Prosecutorial effort under coproduction thus becomes the sum of agency and private litigation that the filing of complaints triggers.

What more specifically defines the EEOC's involvement in these two aspects of coproduction? What are the implications for a White House seeking enforcement reduction via the bureaucracy?

Coproduction Via Complaints

Complaints have largely driven enforcement at the EEOC. Title VII of the Civil Rights Act required the agency to investigate properly filed charges. While state and local fair employment agencies have handled some of these complaints, the EEOC assumed responsibility for most of them. The role of complaints in shaping enforcement has important implications for a White House inclined toward deregulation. Through cutback or other devices, one path to deregulation would be to discourage individuals from filing charges when they perceive discrimination. Lowering the propensity of the populace to complain is, however, far from simple to achieve. It deserves note in this regard that the number of charges filed with the EEOC during the 1970s more than tripled and showed little sign of abating during President Reagan's first term in office (see Table 2).

156   Affirmative Action

An increasing volume of complaints need not be a barrier
to deregulation at the EEOC, however. If the imbalance
between complaints and the agency's ability to investigate and
settle them grows, the EEOC's capacity to establish
enforcement priorities that maximize the agency's impact may
well shrink. As the EEOC attempts to cope with the volume of
complaints, it may devote inadequate attention to the
independent monitoring of its environment--a monitoring that
sheds light on basic patterns of discrimination and helps the
agency target enforcement resources. In essence, excessive
attention to complaint processing can lead to the triumph of
Gresham's law whereby the time spent on trivial cases drives out
the hours needed to pursue important ones (i.e., those that lead
to punishment for the worst offenders and yield a higher return
in terms of inducing compliance). In the abstract, of course, the
EEOC could refuse to let a widening gap between complaints
and resources divert attention from systemic investigations. In
fact, however, powerful forces propel the EEOC toward a
complaint-driven model and make such resistance unlikely.

TABLE 2

CHARGES RECEIVED AT THE
EEOC, FISCAL 1970 - 1983

Fiscal Year	EEOC	State and Local Fair Employment Agencies	Total
1970	15,921	4,201	20,122
1975	31,881	34,216	66,097
1978	37,390	27,189	64,579
1979	35,279	31,290	66,569
1980	45,382	33,486	78,868
1981	56,228	36,989	93,217
1982	54,145	38,255	92,400
1983 (estimate)	66,461	45,737	112,198

Source: Labor Law Reports, Employment Practices 221 (May 20, 1971): 51; 744 (July 9,
1977): 37; 113 (August 19, 1981): 48; 1149 (January 20, 1982): 26; 1172 (April 21, 1982):
32; U.S. House Committee on Appropriations, Department of Commerce, Justice, and
State, The Judiciary, and Related Agencies Appropriations for 1982, Part II (Washington:
U.S. Government Printing Office, 1981), p. 123; Equal Employment Opportunity
Commission, 16th Annual Report 1981 (Washington, 1982); and 17th Annual Report 1982
(Washington, 1983).   U.S. House Committee on Appropriations, Departments of
Commerce, Justice and State, The Judiciary, and Related Agencies Appropriations for
1985, Part 4 (Washington: U.S. Government Printing Office, 1984), pp. 163, 165.

The salience of backlog as a performance indicator deserves particular attention in this regard. This indicator became especially pivotal during the 1970s because of the EEOC's inability to process the growing number of complaints. By the mid-1970s the backlog had mushroomed to over 130,000 (House Com. on Appropriations, 1980: 255), and soon became a symbol of the agency's incompetence. As the Acting Chairman of the EEOC observed in 1981, "We are more sensitive to the question . . . backlogs than perhaps anyone else in the government simply because, unfortunately, that has been the albatross around EEOC's neck. The word 'backlog' is a bugaboo. I wish we could get away from that . . ." He went on to observe that "the whole management scheme that we have in place gears itself toward trying to resolve charges as quickly as possible. We can't win any other way." This observation in part bears testimony to a pervasive cultural norm. As Diver notes, the political audience of a regulatory agency tends to "place a high value on the virtue of responsiveness for its own sake. A policy of ignoring or even deferring complaints appears to offend that value" (Diver, 1980: 275).

Given the potency of backlog as a performance indicator, success in targeting enforcement resources on high-impact, systemic cases largely hinges on the EEOC's ability to process more minor complaints very rapidly. With this in mind, Eleanor Holmes Norton introduced several reforms after she became Chair of the commission in 1977 (House Com. on Educ. and Labor, 1979: 19). Her primary initiative revolved around the introduction of a rapid charge process. Rather than investigate each complaint thoroughly, EEOC personnel would conduct a superficial fact-finding exercise and then attempt to persuade the complainant and employer to reach a no-fault settlement. Simultaneously, the agency would use an Early Litigation Identification Program to single out complaints that might have a large impact for some class of persons. Cases identified under this program would not go through the rapid charge process but would instead receive more intensive investigation. Through these efforts, the EEOC could more readily emphasize the work of the Office of Systemic Programs which conducts extensive investigations leading to major class action suits.

The new procedure helped the EEOC expedite claims processing and reduce the backlog. In fiscal 1979, for instance, the agency settled nearly 50 percent of all complaints through the rapid charge process (General Accounting Office, 1981: 19). By October, 1981, the backlog and shrunk to 16,000 and the average time needed to process some complaints had diminished from 14 to five months (House Com. on Appropriations, 1982: 134). Meanwhile, the EEOC processed some 850 cased under the Early Litigation Identification

Program and initiated some 62 systemic investigations in fiscal 1980 (EEOC, 1980).

Any positive effects of the Norton reforms on the targeting of enforcement resources can, however, be undermined by an increasing imbalance between the volume of complaints and the resources available to handle them. As pressures to process charges mount, legitimate complaints of discrimination may increasingly receive short shrift; investigations may become more and more superficial; the agency may go to greater lengths to persuade complainants to accept modest, no-fault settlements. Ironically, the dynamics unleashed may impair systemic investigations and the targeting of resources. During the early 1980s, for instance, pressures to process charges rapidly reached such heights that certain EEOC employees filed a grievance asserting that they had been asked to dispose of complaints without investigations (Atlanta Constitution, 1984: A). In early 1984, the EEOC General Counsel, David L. Slate complained that pressures to produce quotas of charges processed "continues to be responsible for the greatest diminution ever in this agency's law enforcement. . . efforts" (Atlanta Constituion, 1984: 5A). While EEOC Chairman Clarence Thomas termed this view "hyperbolic," he subsequently acknowledged that the rapid charge system had led to the settlement of some cases "without due regard to the merits or litigation potential of the charge. . .The result was to diminish substantially the pool of adequately investigated charges available for Commission litigation" (House Com. on Appropriations, 1984: 197). Hence, a procedure designed to free agency resources for systemic inquiries began to be a barrier to these investigations.

Enforcement deregulation does not, therefore, hinge upon the ability of the President to reduce complaints. It can also arise in the face of an expanding gap between agency resources and the ability to process charges. Deregulation tends to be served most readily if the agency can settle charges, persuading those with legitimate grievances to accept watered down settlements. To the extent, however, that the backlog begins to grow or complainants feel inadequately served by the EEOC, prosecutorial coproduction may become more evident. This form of coproduction greatly complicates any effort to achieve enforcement reduction.

Prosecutorial Coproduction

From the start, Title VII carved out a role for the private bar in enforcing the law. It explicitly gave complainants the right to sue if the EEOC failed to do so. It authorized the federal court to permit the plaintiff to collect "reasonable" attorney's fees from an employer who had been found guilty of

discrimination.   Thus, it is hardly surprising that "private
General Counselors" have played a major role in enforcing the
law.   In fact, the EEOC files only a small proportion of the
discrimination cases that reach the federal courts. One analysis
completed during the late 1970s found, for instance, that the
percentage of job discrimination suits filed by the EEOC in
federal courts amounted to roughly seven percent of the total
(House Com. on Educ. and Labor, 1979: 462).   Officials at the
EEOC have understood the help that the private bar can provide
and have devoted attention to it.

Other things being equal, the propensity of private lawyers
to become part of an enforcement coalition increases to the
degree that the regulatory agency (a) informs and motivates
complainants to seek help from the private bar, (b) minimizes
information costs for private attorneys, and (c) heightens the
prospects for legal settlements that are financially appealing to
private lawyers.

The EEOC has taken several steps to inform complainants
about the role of the private bar.   Under Eleanor Holmes
Norton, for instance, the agency established the Uniform
Attorney Referral System which attempted to rationalize the
referral process.   This system required that any attorney who
wished to receive referrals from a district office had to file a
form containing information about his or her Title VII
experience and fees.

Of greater significance, the EEOC worked to reduce the
information costs of attorneys who agreed to take
discrimination suits.   Despite Title VII prohibitions against
distributing information obtained in an investigation to the
"public," EEOC officials at an early point decided to furnish
these files to complainants and their attorneys.   This practice
often helped complainants with well-grounded charges find
attorneys who would work for them on a contingent fee basis.
Sensing the value of information as a power resource, several
employers challenged the EEOC practice of opening its
investigatory files.   While the EEOC generally prevailed in the
legal skirmishes it fought with employers over this issue, the
inconsistency of lower court rulings compelled the agency to
follow different policies in different geographic areas. Finally,
in 1981 the Supreme Court in EEOC v. Associated Dry Goods
Corp. upheld the agency practice of divulging this information.
In reaching this decision, the majority opinion underscored that
private litigation remained an integral part of the Title VII
enforcement scheme and that the poor complainant in particular
would suffer if denied this information (Yamachika, 1982: 816-
849).   In addition to releasing files, the EEOC attempted to
reduce information costs for the private bar in other ways.
Under the Area Bar Center Program, for instance, the EEOC

established litigation support centers to update the private bar on significant developments in Title VII laws, and to provide more specific technical assistance to private lawyers who requested consultation.

Finally, the regulatory agency may increase the financial appeal of settlements. One EEOC effort in this regard involved risk reduction through a subsidy program. During the Norton years, the EEOC experimented with an Attorney Revolving Fund Program whereby in selected areas the agency lent certain lawyers (especially minorities) money to cover some of the initial costs in preparing a Title VII case. The attorney would have to repay the loan only if he or she won the case and received reimbursement from the court. The EEOC also tended to be liberal in certifying charges for class action. Class actions not only possess appeal as a mechanism for achieving broader social reforms; lawyers tend to prefer such cases because their remuneration will probably be greater if a court decides in favor of a whole class rather than an individual (Rutherglen, 1980: 688-741).

A President bent on deregulation can attempt to disrupt the EEOC's efforts to facilitate prosecutorial coproduction. For instance, the agency will obviously have fewer files of pertinent information to turn over to private lawyers if its capacity to conduct investigations diminishes. This development could exact a particular hardship on the poor who can seldom pay for attorneys out of their own pockets. Even if the White House makes the EEOC less helpful to the private bar, however, statutory guarantees governing individual access to the courts seem likely to lead to considerable litigation. This raises the possibility of a kind of regulatory Catch-22--that reduced enforcement at the EEOC could spawn an increase in litigation by individual complainants. It deserves note in this regard that while the number of suits filed by the EEOC during the initial years of the Reagan Administration declined, the number of employment discrimination cases initiated in U.S. District courts grew by 24 percent during President Reagan's first year in office (EEOC, 1982: 228).

Given the potential for private litigation to fill the gap left by enforcement deregulation at the EEOC, a White House might in the abstract conceive of a preemptive strategy to foster deregulation. This approach would imply buttressing rather than cutting the EEOC's resources. The utility of this strategy becomes evident if one considers the optimum level of enforcement under a system featuring the coproduction of sanctions. At least from one perspective, this optimum would exist if the EEOC prosecuted valid cases that would not be pursued at all or as effectively by the private bar. As a corollary, the agency would refrain from suits that the private sector would and could handle just as, if not more, effectively. The preemptive approach to deregulation emphasizes undermining this optimum. The EEOC would work on cases best left to the private sector, attempting to settle them with more modest penalties than would apply if the private bar were involved. In the meantime cases that the EEOC alone might usefully pursue would be left to languish before an indifferent private bar. Attractive as this preemptive strategy might be, however, it calls for a level of information and finely tuned deregulation levers that the White House simply does not possess.

IMPLICATIONS

Enforcement deregulation at the EEOC can assume many guises. It unfolds when the agency obtains less information or loses the capacity to synthesize it into usable knowledge. It surfaces when the regulatory bureaucracy insists on more proof to conclude that discrimination has occurred. It emerges when the agency inflicts less severe penalties and demands less in the way of corrective action from offending employers. Given these characteristics, to what degree can the White House foster enforcement deregulation via the bureaucracy? This analysis suggests that the deregulation levers available to the White House are error prone in the case of the EEOC. Through budget control, prosecutorial dependence and personnel appointments (or turmoil over them), the President can trigger some enforcement deregulation. But prospects for unanticipated consequences loom large. The presence of an independent commission, a full-fledged representative bureaucracy, as well as a regulatory technology featuring complaint-driven and prosecutorial coproduction all complicate matters. Success in fostering enforcement deregulation at the EEOC may backfire as the private bar compensates by unleashing new initiatives to enforce the law.

This essay comprises only an initial step in dissecting the relationship between different kinds of White House initiatives and modification in EEOC enforcement. Important research tasks await. For instance, students of the subject need to measure enforcement deregulation more precisely. Given the subtle and multidimensional character of such deregulation, developing accurate indicators of the phenomenon will be a major challenge. Aside from efforts to gauge and explain enforcement, research needs to probe the ramifications of enforcement deregulation for compliance. The forces that lead members of a target group to comply with a law are complex. Some employers obey because they believe in the reasonableness of the law or the legitimacy of the decision process that produced it. Those who fail to comply may do so for reasons of

162   Affirmative Action

limited capacity rather than obstinacy. For those interested in
the broader importance of deregulation via the bureaucracy,
estimating the amount of variance in compliance accounted for
by enforcement effort is a central, if Sisyphean, task.

A firmer grasp of the relationship between enforcement
and compliance can ultimately illuminate the broader role of the
President in regulatory arenas. Above all, it can clarify the
degree to which the chief executive can discourage compliance
without inducing enforcement deregulation. It seems highly
probable that the President through rhetoric and other actions
can do much to create the illusion of deregulation. Key groups
may come to feel less regulated when in fact they are not;
opponents of fair employment practices may thereby become
emboldened. The perception of diminished enforcement
(whether well grounded in reality or not) appears to have
emerged under the Reagan Administration. In 1983, for
example, Clarence Thomas, Chairman of the EEOC,
acknowledged that much of the public believed that the Reagan
Administration had reduced enforcement of equal employment
laws. Thomas noted that this perception prompted many
employers to express surprise when EEOC personnel called to
investigate a complaint. According to him, their response was
often, "Why are you guys doing this? I thought civil rights was
on the back burner" (Chronicle of Higher Educ., 1983: 9). Thus,
the President may discourage compliance and foster a sense of
freedom from regulatory burdens even when his capacity to
direct and control enforcement deregulation via the bureaucracy
remains quite constrained.

REFERENCES

Atlanta Constitution. 1984. (January 14, 1984): 1A.

Atlanta Constitution. 1984. (February 14, 1984): 5A.

Chronicle of Higher Education (June 8, 1983): 9.

Diver, Colin S. "A Theory of Regulatory Enforcement." Public
    Policy 28 (Summer, 1980): 287-288.

Heclo, Hugh. 1977. A Government of Strangers (Washington:
    Brookings Institution.

Moe, Terry M. "Regulatory Performance and Presidential
    Administration." American Journal of Political Science 46
    (May, 1982): 197.

Romzek, Barbara S. and Hendricks, J. Stephen ."Organizational Involvement and Representative Bureaucracy: Can We Have It Both Ways?" American Political Science Review 76 (March, 1982): 75-82.

Rutherglen, George. "Title VII Class Actions." University of Chicago Law Review 47 (Summer, 1980): 688-741.

Thompson, Frank T. "Deregulation by the Bureaucracy: OSHA and the Augean Quest for Error Correction." Public Administration Review 42 (May/June, 1982): 202-212.

Washington Council of Lawyers, Reagan Civil Rights: The First Twenty Months (Washington: unpublished paper, 1983).

This definition in part derives from Gordon P. Whitaker, "Coproduction: Citizen Participation in Service Delivery." Public Administration Review 40 (May/June, 1980): 240-246.

Yamachika, Thomas. "Beyond Equal Employment Opportunity Commission v. Associated Dry Goods Corporation: A New Defense of the EEOC's Role in the Title VII Enforcement Process." California Law review 70 (May, 1982): 816-849.

See especially Yin, Robert K. "Studying the Implementation of Public Programs." In Studying Implementation: Methodological and Administrative Issues (Chatham, N.J.: Chatham House, 1982), pp. 36-72.

U. S. Equal Employment Opportunity Commission, 15th Annual Report, 1980 (Washington, 1981), pp. 26-28.

These data on EEOC suits come from U.S. Equal Employment Commission Annual Reports for Fiscal 1974 and 1981, a phone interview with EEOC staff conducted in February 1983, and the Annual Report of the Director of the Administrative Office of the United States Courts, 1981 (Washington: U. S. Government Printing Office, 1982), p. 228.

U. S. General Accounting Office, Further Improvements Needed In EEOC Enforcement Activities (Washington: HRD-81-29, 1981), p. 5.

U. S. House Committee on Appropriations, Departments of State, Justice, and Commerce, The Judiciary, and Related Agencies Appropriations for 1981, Part 8 (Washington: U.S. Government Printing Office, 1980), p. 255.

U. S. House Committee on Appropriations, <u>Departments of Commerce, Justice and State, The Judiciary, and Related Agencies Appropriations for 1982, Part II</u> (Washington: U. S. Government Printing Office, 1981), p. 190.

U. S. House Committee on Appropriations, <u>Departments of Commerce. . .for 1982, Part II</u>, p. 134.

U. S. House Committee on Appropriations, <u>Departments of Commerce, Justice, and State, The Judiciary, and Related Agencies Appropriations for 1985, Part 4</u> (Washington: U. S. Government Printing Office, 1984), p. 197.

U. S. House Committee on Education and Labor, <u>Oversight on Federal Enforcement of Equal Employment Opportunity Laws</u> (Washington: U. S. Government Printing Office, 1979), p. 19.

U. S. Senate Committee on Labor and Human Resources, <u>Nominations: William M. Bell,</u> . . .(Washington: U.S. Government Printing Office, 1981), p. 28.

U. S. Senate Committee on Labor and Human Resources, <u>Nomination, Clarence Thomas</u> . . .(Washington: U. S. Government Printing Office, 1982), p. 16.

Michael B. Preston

Affirmative Action Policy:
Can It Survive the Reaganites?

The struggle for equal employment opportunities in America has had a rather checkered past marked by periods of great strides forward followed by decades of little or no progress. Even a brief overview of the history involved shows the depth and breadth of the controversy, a conflict in which everyone, particularly the officials and agencies of the federal government, must eventually take sides. At times in our history, the federal government has avidly supported and encouraged discrimination; at other times, it has been a leader in the battle for equal opportunity. No administration since the inception of the affirmative action program, however, has reacted more negatively to it than has the Reagan Administration. Leading government officials, backed by Reagan, are attacking the policy on all fronts. Although such formidable opposition has led some supporters of the affirmative action program to expect its swift demise, the basic question is not whether or not affirmative action will survive the Reaganites but what the cost of that tenuous survival will be. At best, the policy will be watered down and enforcement is likely to be reduced. Even worse, however, Reagan's antagonistic attitude toward affirmative action may indicate to employers, especially those who are hostile to the program to begin with, that they can halt their compliance procedures and be relatively safe from governmental reprisal. The attacks on affirmative action policy by the Reagan Administration have been fairly comprehensive.

The Challenges to Affirmative Action Policy

If one could predict anything about the 1980 election, it was that if Ronald Reagan was elected, civil rights gains won in

165

the past would have to be protected in the future. It did not take extraordinary vision to come to this conclusion; the Republican platform and the rhetoric of the candidate made that clear during the campaign. What was not clear is how soon and in what ways the attack would take place if he were elected. The strategy that is currently being employed is the subject of intense debate by civil rights forces and their allies.

The opening-round of the debate on affirmative action policy was put forth by the Heritage Foundation, a conservative think tank. They urged Reagan to challenge court ordered affirmative action policy. The administration's chief civil rights enforcer, William French Smith, agreed but wanted to wait until there was a clear Supreme Court ruling against affirmative action policy (Champaign-Urbana News Gazette 1/17/83). The Heritage Foundation argued that "because groups of past victims rather than individual victims are given preference, affirmative action imposes an unjust burden on the innocent students, workers and firms who through no fault of their own must now suffer" (Champaign-Urbana News Gazette 1/17/83). They go on to argue that remedies should apply only to individual victims, not to all members of the victimized groups.

Civil rights groups on the other hand, argue the need for broad remedies "because it is hard to identify all individual victims of group discrimination, and because the remedies only deprive non-victims of benefits they would not have had but for the discrimination" (Champaign-Urbana News Gazette 1/17/83).

The second issue revolves around the amount of influence President Reagan has over the Civil Rights Commission. He has now appointed five (5) persons to the six (6) member commission, including a black, Chairman Clarence Pendleton. Advocates of the commission fear that it will lose its autonomy because so many of the appointees are being replaced. Given some of Pendleton's views, they have a right to be concerned. He has stated that "affirmative action with its goals and preferences is a bankrupt policy because it often leads to an emphasis on statistical parity rather than equal opportunity" (N.Y. Times, 10/3/82). The recent restructuring of the Commission has not changed much because with the cooperation of Senate Republicans, Reagan still appointed people very much opposed to affirmative action policy.

The third issue concerns the Reagan administration's attack on affirmative action (AA) policy regarding employment. At issue here is a new set of regulations that would have, according to civil rights groups, exempted 80 percent of colleges and universities from having to write AA plans. The hostility toward these new regulations by civil rights groups, some business leaders and others caused the Administration to delay publication of these regulations which would have sharply curtailed the Labor Department's oversight of federal contractors, including colleges and universities (Labor Rel. in Educ. Newsletter, 1982).

The fourth issue relates to the Justice Department's opposition to changes in the last hired, first fired system. After the 1984 Supreme Court decision rejecting a layoff plan based on an AA consent decree involving Memphis firemen, civil rights and labor attorney Douglas Seaver observed: "no sooner had the Supreme Court's decision been issued than William Bradford Reynolds, head of the Justice Department's Civil Rights division, announced that he would order the review and assess the validity of hundreds of court-ordered affirmative action programs where the courts had employed racial quotas and goals in hiring to effectuate appropriate relief" (N.Y. Times 2/17/83).

The fifth issue is of special concern because it has to do with white perceptions of black opportunity. A recent study by Elliot Smith of Purdue University and James Kluegel of the University of Illinois shows that most whites believe blacks have better than average employment opportunities due to reverse discrimination. They found that most Americans see their own opportunities as good and expect this is similar for blacks; indeed, the media's portrayal of blacks is the only exposure many whites have to blacks so they see an unrealistic portrayal of blacks as either policemen or doctors (National Leader, 2/17/83). The clear implication here is that if people perceive blacks as having opportunity, why support AA polices?

In recent months, the rhetoric of the administration is now being matched with reality. Action is now being taken which challenges the need for AA policy in a wide-range of areas. A brief discussion of the definition of the concept will set the stage for the confrontation that follows.

The Concept: Pro and Con

In 1941, President Roosevelt issued the first Executive Order that dealt with equal opportunity in employment. The order forbade employment discrimination on the basis of race, creed, color or national origin by employers who held Defense Department contracts. Subsequent Executive Orders broadened the scope of the anti-discrimination clause to include all employers receiving federal funds but it was not until twenty years after Roosevelt's order that the idea of affirmative action became interwoven with the discrimination ban. President Kennedy, in issuing Executive Order 10925, included the following statement:

> "The contractor will take affirmative action to ensure that applicants are employed...without regard to their race,

creed, color or national origin" (House
subcommittee Report, 1982:5).

Unfortunately, however, neither this order nor its successors
defined the phrase "affirmative action" or outlined how such a
program would be implemented. Meanwhile, Congress enacted
legislation guaranteeing the right to equal employment
opportunity. The 1964 Civil Rights Act included provisions
banning discrimination, even on the basis of gender, in an effort
to promote a sense of "color-blindness" in hiring situation.
Again, though, no concrete implementation plans were suggested
and it was left to the Department of Labor (DOL) and the Equal
Employment Opportunity Commission (EEOC) to structure the
procedural aspect and enforce the rather nebulous concepts of
"equal opportunity" and "affirmative action."
    Finally, in 1971, employers received some guidance when
the DOL issued Order 4 which defined an affirmative action
program as "a set of specific and result-oriented procedures to
which a contractor commits itself to apply every good faith
effort" (Fed. Reg. 1970: 2586, 2587). The order also concludes
that "an acceptable affirmative action program must include an
analysis of areas within which the contractor is deficient in the
utilization of minority groups, and, further, goals and timetables
to which the contractor's good faith efforts must be directed to
correct these deficiencies" (Fed. Reg. 1970: 2587). In 1971, the
DOL, in an attempt to refine the definition, explained that the
term "underutilization" meant "having fewer minorities or
women in a particular job classification than would reasonably
be expected by their availability" (41C. F.R. 60.2.11).
    Almost immediately, the controversy began, and it
continues. Opponents of the affirmative action program claim
that the DOL's order requires the employers to use a "quota"
system, i.e. hiring a specific number of minorities and women
thereby excluding white males from consideration for those
jobs. They argue that the legislative history of the Civil Rights
bill shows that Congress specifically rejected a system by which
minorities and women would get "preferential treatment" in
favor of laws which only prohibits the employer from
discriminating against these groups. Furthermore, they contend
that an essential element of a violation under the 1964 bill was
the "intent to discriminate" and that this crucial element has
been totally eliminated by the DOL orders which compel
scrutiny only of the results of the employer's hiring procedures.
In their view, the affirmative action plans presently required by
the EEOC concentrate too much of the effects of discrimination
in direct contradiction to the purpose of the Civil Rights bill
which was to remedy the effects of discrimination only by
outlawing discrimination itself (Capaldi, 1980: 42).

Other people are dissatisfied with the affirmative action policy because they feel it does more harm than good. On a strictly economic basis, compliance costs can be high; in 1977 alone, the cost of meeting the EEOC's regulations for private companies was 4.34 billion dollars (Hatch, 1980: 33). It has also been suggested that by setting employment standards on the basis of race or sex rather than ability, employers are slowly eroding the market value of the labor of the individual worker. Since chance of employment, and often subsequent promotions and pay raises, are unrelated to the worker's skills, those skilled workers not belonging to a minority group find that their skills have devalued (Hatch, 1980: 35). On a "psycho-sociological" basis, it has been claimed that the existence of affirmative action programs harms minorities, and blacks in particular, by negatively influencing their own estimation of self-worth and their acceptance by their peers in the working world. According to this theory, affirmative action programs create the impression that the achievements of minorities have been conferred by reluctant employers rather than earned by the individual (Sowell, 1976: 47). Some observers also contend that the programs have created more social problems for black workers since it has set them apart and barred the natural and gradual assimilation into American society that has seemingly worked well for other ethnic and racial groups.

Although there was and is a great deal of opposition to the DOL's implementation of affirmative action policy, there are many supporters of it who feel that the program has only begun the attempt to correct the abysmal employment situation faced by women and minorities in America today. They claim that opponents of the affirmative action programs are ignoring several crucial realities when they denounce the manner in which the program is run. First, there is not a "quota" system forcing employers to hire unqualified minority workers in order to meet standards set by the EEOC. Even in 1971, when the DOL first issued its definition of underutilization, it was recognized that the affirmative action program "does not command that any persons be hired simply because he was formerly the subject of discrimination or because he is a member of a minority group...the Congress did not intend... to guarantee a job to every person regardless of qualifications" (Griggs V. Duke Power Co., 401 U.S. 424 (1981)). An affirmative action plan is simply a convenient way for an employer to compare the number of minority workers he presently employs in any given job skill classification with the number of available minority workers who would be qualified for that classification; if there is an unacceptable gap between the two, the employer must outline the methods he plans to use to reduce and/or eliminate the discrepancy.

Second, the use of goals and timetables within a plan is simply a means of helping the employer carry out the plan by measuring its progress. Methods of progress measurement are commonly used in business enterprises and can be as helpful in judging the effectiveness of personnel policies as in judging the sales record of a new product. As noted by George Sape of Organization Resources Counselors, Inc., "there is nothing unusual about...the use of a measurement system...(I) would find it surprising if a larger number of corporate organizations would oppose the existence of some kind of numerical measurement" (House Subcommittee Report, 1982: 20). Third, the concept of requiring proof of intent to discriminate does not deal with the very real problem of minority workers not applying for jobs with a specific company because of its reputation for discrimination against them. Additionally, since the highest court in the nation has ruled that "Congress directed the thrust of the (Civil Rights) act to the consequence of employment practices, not simply the motivation," there is no basis for the claims that the DOL is erroneously applying the law (Griggs v. Duke Power Co., 40 U. S. 426).

To those that bewail the cost and paperwork involved with compliance, advocates of the policies point out that there are always a certain number of "strings" attached to any federal contract and that the time and money spent on affirmative action constitute only a fraction of the cost of running any business. They also contend that the affirmative action programs are necessary to counteract the years of discrimination suffered by the minorities, usually at the hands of the government or with the blessings of its laws and courts. Since the position of minorities in this country today is "the tragic but inevitable consequence of centuries of unequal treatment," they argued that the small cost burden is almost irrelevant (Regents of the University of California v. Bakke 438 U.S. 428, 1976).

Few people, however, seriously contend that equal employment opportunity laws are no longer necessary. The controversy instead centers around how to prevent discrimination in employment. The major battle is focused upon the use of standards by which an employer's progress toward equal opportunity is measured; for many people, these standards are, for all practical purposes, "quotas" which in their view cannot be tolerated. Those having this opinion often blame past presidential administrations for allowing the DOL to institute a "quota" system and look to the Reagan Administration to come down squarely on their side and champion their struggle against affirmative action. After all, the 1980 Republican Presidential platform stated that "equal opportunity should not be jeopardized by bureaucratic regulations and decisions which rely on quotas, ratios and numerical requirements to exclude some individuals in favor of others" (Seligman, 1982: 144). This statement was interpreted as a promise that if Reagan were elected the affirmative action program would be radically changed, if not totally abolished.

Upon election, Reagan's first problem was to find someone to chair the EEOC who shared his belief in the injustice of the "quota" system. After a couple of false starts, he finally appointed Clarence Thomas to the position. When questioned about his views on the affirmative action policy, Thomas stated "I'm not that wedded to restricting myself to ratios, rigid goals and timetables. I just don't think they have worked that well" ("Interview," 1982: 5). Neither Reagan nor Thomas, however, elaborated on what type of enforcement policies they did favor.

The first indication of the direction in which the Administration would try to change the affirmative action program came in August, 1981. Explaining that the cost of compliance had become too burdensome for small companies, the DOL proposed several revisions of their current regulations. The most dramatic change was the proposal to raise the thresholds which governed affirmative action plan preparation requirements for non-construction contractors and subcontractors. Under the previous system, an employer with at least 50 employees and a contract with the federal government for $50,000 or more, is required to file details of the affirmative action plan with the DOL and be subject to spot checks and scheduled compliance reviews. The new proposals raised the employee standard to 250 and the monetary standard to $1 million. Additionally, the proposals deleted the requirement of aggregation of the dollar amounts of all the contracts made with the employer during a given year to determine whether or not the employer meets the threshold. According to current figures, the raised thresholds would exempt almost 75% of the companies now holding contracts with the federal government (Seligman, 1982: 156).

The proposed revisions also contained other procedural changes for companies that would still be covered by the affirmative action plan requirements. A contractor who employed between 250-499 employees could prepare an abbreviated plan which would be less inclusive and detailed than the currently required plans. Additionally, any employer could develop a plan that would cover a five year time period; by doing so, he would gain two benefits. First, the employer protects himself from any and all spot reviews. Second, and more importantly, certain complaints would be investigated on the facts stated in the complaint only; there would be no investigation of possible widespread discriminatory practices. A corollary of this procedure would be that complaints could only be made on an individual basis and not on behalf of a group or class. According to the DOL, the purpose of the abbreviated and five year plan options was to promote voluntary compliance with the affirmative action program.

The public comment and controversy aroused by the publication of the DOL proposals prompted the House of Representatives to form a subcommittee on employment opportunities. During the subcommittee's hearings, Administration officials repeatedly testified to changes in both procedure and policy designed to end the "quota" system. Malcolm Lovell, Under Secretary of the DOL, stated that "although we will continue to require contractors to set goals where there is not reasonable utilization of the available minorities or women, we will not insist on or support anything that operates as a quota...preferential treatment or quotas-- including measures by another name that constitutes quotas-- (these) are not proper or defensible" (House Subcommittee Report, 1982: 12). Earlier during the same set of hearings, William Bradford Reynolds, Assistant Attorney General for Civil Rights, had stated a similar Justice department policy toward "quotas" saying that no system "designed to provide nonvictims of discrimination or preferential treatment" would be supported (House Subcommittee Report, 1982: 12). He added that his department would no longer seek sex or race conscious remedies in cases dealing with unlawful employment discrimination (House Subcommittee Report, 1982: 12, 18).

In 1981, then, there didn't seem to be any real changes in the basic operation of the EEOC or the affirmative action program. In August, 1981, the DOL withdrew its proposed revisions and it is not expected that they will be reissued in the near future. Does this mean, then, that the Reagan Administration really poses no threat to the affirmative action program? Is it in danger or not?

In Defense of AA Policy

On the one hand, the affirmative action program is not doomed to extinction regardless of what Reagan says or does. It cannot be abolished without alienating both the people who benefit from it and the people who support its purpose and goals. Even the business community is not totally against the affirmative action program. Although there are a multitude of complaints about the compliance procedures, witnesses before the House subcommittee "concurred that there continue to be a need for goals and timetables and noted that they are a valuable management tool" (House Subcommittee Report, 1982: 20). For many companies, the continuance of the program is more desirable than having to write off as a total loss the time and money invested in developing and maintaining their plans.

Additionally, there is a growing appreciation of the benefits that can accrue to a company because of its affirmative action programs. First, there is a public relations aspect in that a company must sell either its product or itself in order to be successful; a positive image in all areas, including employment opportunities, is crucial. Second, the implementation of affirmative action programs usually involves an improvement in personnel and management techniques. Dr. Bernard Anderson, commenting on the ATT-EEOC consent decree, said "The consent decree was the catalyst necessary to spur the company toward many positive changes in personnel policies that top management today lauds as beneficial to the firm. The more efficient and equitable personnel section...puts the telephone company in a much stronger position to compete with other firms" (House Subcommittee Report, 1982: 17).

However, just because the affirmative action program has its supporters does not mean that one can dismiss the Reagan Administration's attempt to restructure the program as an insubstantial and futile word game. In many instances, what is said can have as much effect as what is done. Many observers fear that what Reagan has accomplished in the past two years is to foster an attitude of indifference and a feeling that violations of the affirmative action laws will, for the most part, be ignored by the governmental enforcement agencies.

There are some indications that this subtle erosion of the affirmative action program is working. It is generally agreed that compliance reviews are being made less frequently and that the rules are applied less strictly than before Reagan was elected. It is also obvious to those within the EEOC that commitment to the goals of the affirmative action program has been weakened and that employers sense the more lenient attitude and act accordingly. For example, many universities are now shifting to open recruitment as a way to avoid hiring minorities and women, and while this is legal, the hostile attitude displayed by some department heads towards AA policy becomes clearly evident.

It is possible that the Administration's attitude toward affirmative action, ranging as it does from apathy to hostility, may be more destructive than any changes in the structure and procedures of the program would be. Proposals for change can be fought through political pressure and legislation; on the other hand it is next to impossible to effectively fight the growth of an attitude. The greatest fear is that the less stringent enforcement brought about by negative attitude will result in an upsurge of discriminatory practice by employers. Even with the relatively stringent enforcement that took place during the 1970 s, discrimination was prevalent. According to a recent report, black workers made fewer gains in the employment field during the 1970s than they had in the previous decade (Wescot, 1980). Many local governments allocate only minimal resources to their affirmative action programs and that the program administrations are often woefully uninformed about compliance regulations and agencies. Administration officials say that they hope to promote voluntary compliance but unfortunately "past experience indicates that elimination of job segregation for women and minorities on a voluntary basis was meaningless until a strong enforcement program, including affirmative action and goals and timetables, provided an incentive for action" (House Subcommittee Report, 1982: 46). One problem with reliance on voluntary compliance was highlighted in a study designed to test the correlation between the attitudes of personnel managers and their implementation of affirmative action programs. Although the managers strongly believed that employers have a responsibility to hire blacks and other minorities, they also rated blacks as undesirable employees who could only perform at the lowest level jobs (manuscript submitted, Journal of Urban Affairs). It is obvious that a conflict exists between these two beliefs and without EEOC enforcement, minorities lose.

This conflict has also been reflected in recent public opinion polls which indicate that a majority of the people surveyed no longer support affirmative action programs. The results of one survey, conducted to verify an earlier 1980 Gallup poll, led to the conclusion that "belief in individualism, an antipathy to preferential treatment and devotion to the principle of achievement though merit rather than ascription privilege prove to be stronger influences on public opinion than dedication to affirmative action programs" (Sackett, 1980: 9).

On a more theoretical level, there is also a good argument that the affirmative action program is, indeed, in trouble. Burton Clark has theorized that there are certain factors necessary for the stability of any program which reflects a societal value, in this case reparation for past employment discrimination. The first factor involves the manner in which the value is defined, i.e., whether or not it is embodied in the goals and standards of a group committed to its success. Additionally, the stability of a program depends on the relative social position of the person who is responsible for its implementation; if they have little or no power, the programs may be consistently challenged. Finally, the program needs to reflect values that are acceptable to and supported by the general population (Clark, 1965: 159-167).

When each of these determinants of stability is applied to the affirmative action program, it is clear that the program is well on its way to becoming, in Clark's terms, a "precarious value." Although the EEOC does have regulations and standards, enforcement is becoming lax and violations are often not dealt

with properly. This growing disparity between what is said and
what is done will result in a more loosely defined set of rules
and less commitment to those rules. In the same way, as the
Administration denigrates the objectives and procedures of the
EEOC, they are also weakening the influence of the officials
within the agency. Perhaps most frightening to the advocates of
affirmative action, however, is the fact the public in general has
begun to express dissatisfaction with both the program and the
rationale behind it.

     Another method of ascertaining both the stability and the
effectiveness of a government program or agency is to measure
the relative strength of its allies and foes. The present
affirmative action program has staunch supporters that can be
divided into two basic categories. The first includes
organizations such as unions, women's groups and certain
legislators and governmental officials. These supporters all
have varying degrees of political power but the characteristic
they share is that their main purpose is not ensuring the success
of affirmative action; affirmative action is merely a part of
their political and sociological ideology and, as such, their
involvement with and support of the program is limited. There
are organizations devoted to the support and growth of the
affirmative action program, such as human and civil rights
groups, but these groups often have little political power. They
are effective in publicizing potential threats to the program but
cannot really marshall the forces necessary to defeat the
opposition. Those opponents, on the other hand, include many
business organizations, academics, political groups and the
reigning Administration. Even the chairman of the EEOC has
spoken out against the very policies and procedures he is
supposed to be enforcing. Reagan and his appointees wield
tremendous political clout and are in a position to totally
dismantle the affirmative action program. At present, even the
economic situation and the judicial system are negating some of
the progress that has been made. As unemployment rises, so,
too, does resentment against perceived "preferential
treatment."

     In the judicial arena, two 1984 Supreme Court decisions
have undercut some of the gains of AA plans; these decisions,
coupled with Reagan's appointments of several federal court
judges, indicate that the administration's attitude has
penetrated the judiciary. When the strength of the allies is
compared to the strength of the opponents, the conclusion is
inescapable. Affirmative action programs are headed for
some very rough times.

     The 1984 Supreme Court decision in Memphis, Grove City,
and, to a lesser extent Boston, permit the administration to
actively attack specific AA plans in conjunction with their

policy of inaction. In the Memphis case, the Court held invalid a layoff plan which circumvented various seniority privileges in order to preserve the goals of the city's AA plan. The Court held that "...Title VII protects bona fide seniority systems, and it is inappropriate to deny an innocent employee the benefits of his seniority in order to provide a remedy in a pattern of practice suit such as this" (<u>Firefighters Local Union No. 1784 v. Statts</u> No. 82-206, Slip op. 1984, 12). Even if the provision of Title VII had been ignored--as the concurring and dissenting opinions suggested--the Court found that the consent decree itself would not permit the layoff plan. Barring express language to the contrary, the Court would not assume that the city would ignore the seniority system in a decree to which union members and non-minorities were not parties. The majority apparently rejected the dissent's observation that "particularly in civil rights litigation in which implementation of a consent decree often takes years, such foresight is unattainable" (Blackmun, Dissent, at 17). Within weeks, two federal judges--in Newark and Cincinnati--relied on the Memphis decision to strike down layoff plans resembling the Memphis one (Public Adm. Times, 1984: 3). A similar case occurred in Boston. The Supreme Court vacated a lower court ruling which upheld a Memphis type layoff plan; the Court remanded the case for a consideration of mootness based on recent legislation in Boston which provided revenue to rehire laid off employees and maintain in minimum staffing level in the future (Neeley, 1984: 1772).

The <u>Grove City</u> case, limiting the federal government's role in Title IX (20 U.S.C. 1681 (1976)) sex discrimination suits, will have similar impact on race discrimination suits since Title IX mirrors Title VII (42 U.S.C. 2000 et seq. (1976)) which proscribes racial and ethnic discrimination where federal funds are involved (<u>Grove City College v. Bell</u>, No. 82-792, Slip op., 1984). Findings that the funds received by Grove City College reached only one program, the financial aid program, the Court held that Title IX sanctions and remedies reach only the affected program rather than the entire institution. This analysis makes the dubious assumption that the impact of federal funds is limited to only one program; this seems particularly weak given the close relation and interdependence between college departments and programs (Grove City College, v. Bell, 1984). As the dissent noted, (Brennan, Dissenting at 21) this stance will allow an entity receiving federal funds to discriminate in some spheres of its activities by claiming that this facet of their operation is not a beneficiary of federal funds.

Conclusion
        Surprisingly enough, it is the critics of the affirmative
action program who seem to be dejectedly forcecasting its
continued growth and success. Apparently, there is a general
feeling among them that "it seems safe to say that racial and
sexual quotas are solidly established in our midst and will remain
so for the foreeable future. Indeed, nothing less than serious
social upheaval or major constitutional crisis--certainly not
mere change of administrations or shift in the balance of
congressional power--is apt to dislodge them" (Decter, 1980:
65). It is important to note, however, that these critics are
usually concerned about the Reagan Administration's failure to
make major policy and procedural changes. When judging the
effectiveness of Reagan's tactic in his fight against affirmative
action, it is crucial to understand that he is directing his
attention to thousands of small companies which are not
benefiting from affirmative action programs in the way large
corporations are; many of these employers have always been
hostile to the idea of affirmative action and have only instituted
and maintained programs because they are forced to.   The
Reagan Administration's attitude has convinced these employers
that violations of the EEOC regulations will basically go
unnoticed.   Some   employers   may   even   perceive   the
Administration's stance as permission to completely disregard
their own affirmative action plans. After all, they can find no
valid reason for continuing their programs. They never saw the
carrot; now, they no longer need fear the stick.
        In the final analysis, the Reagan Administration's
continuing policy of lax enforcement of civil rights law coupled
with their recent "victories" in the Court have at least posed
significant threats to the viability of AA plans and may well
have encouraged the abandonment of such efforts. While it is
difficult to guage precisely the consequences of Reagan's policy
of inaction, the Memphis decision has already produced a very
active and threatening policy toward AA programs. Within four
months the Justice Department has intervened in four cases
involving consent decrees, instigated a review of all government
anti-discrimination agreements to see if they use "quotas"
(Neeley, 1984: 1772-74). On the other hand, Grove City
generated a Congressional response. Efforts to legislatively
"reverse" that decision were unavailing, however, as Senator
Hatch threatened to propose 1,300 amendments to the bill, and
supporters were forced to withdraw the bill for the session (N.Y.
Times, 10/3/84). And for these and other reasons, both the
political and social climate today make the survival of AA
policy "precarious."

REFERENCES

"Affirmative Action." The Washington Monthly, January 1981.

Capaldi, Nicholas. "Twisting the Law." Policy Review, 12 (Summer 1980) pp. 65-72.

"Civil Rights Plan Tied to Fund Bill Shelved in Senate." New York Times, October 3, 1984.

Clark, Burton R. "Organizational Adaptation and Precarious Values." Complex Organizations: A Sociological Reader, Amitai Etzioni. ed. New York: Holt Rinehart Winston, 1965, pp. 159-167.

Cooper, Charles. "Two Cheers for Quotas--and a Resounding Boo." Report from the Center for Philosophy and Public Policy, 2 (Summer 1982) pp. 9-10.

Decter, Midge. "Benign Victimization." Policy Review, 13 (Summer 1980) pp. 5-72.

Equal Employment Opportunity Commission. "Affirmative Action and Equal Employment; A Guidebook for Employers." 1974.

"Every Man for Himself." Time, September 7, 1981.

Griggs v. Duke Power, 401 U.S. 424, 915 S. Ct. 849, (1971).

Hatch, Orrin. "Loading the Economy." Policy Review 12 (Spring 1980) pp. 23-37.

"Interview." Labor Relations in Education, July 1982.

Johnson, Carmen. "League Submits Comments on OFCCP Rules: Opposes Relaxation of Affirmative Action Requirements." National Urban League Point, November/December, 1981.

Johnson, Carmen. "What Happened to Those Regulations?" Labor Relations in Education, August 16, 1982.

"Labor's Affirmative Action Proposals Now on Hold." Labor Relations in Education, August 16, 1982.

Neely, Anthony. "Government Role in Routing out, Remedying Discrimination is Shifting." National Journal. September 22, 1984, p. 1772-74.

Michael B. Preston   179

Regents of the University of California v. Bakke, 438 U.S. 265
    (1978).

Sackett, Victoria. "Ignoring the People." Policy Review, 12
    (Spring 1980) 9-22.

Seligman, Daniel. "Affirmative Action Is Here to Stay.
    Fortune, April 19 1982.

Sowell, Thomas. "Affirmative Action Reconsidered." The
    Public Interest, 42 (Winter, 1976) pp. 43-54.

"Understanding Affirmative Action," unpublished manuscript,
    submitted to Journal of Urban Affairs.

United States Commission on Civil Rights. Affirmative Action
    in the 1980's: Dismantling the Process of Discrimination.
    November 1981.

United States Congress, House Representatives, Committee on
    Education and Labor, subcommittee on Employment
    Opportunities. Report on Affirmative Action and the
    Federal Enforcement of Equal Employment Opportunity
    Laws. Washington, D.C.: GPO, 1982.

Westcott, Diane Nilsen. Monthly Labor Review, June 1980.

"White House Record on Minority Hiring." U.S. News and World
    Report, May 11, 1981.

Index

Adams, C. 130, 141
Affirmative Action: American values and 2; anti-discrimination and 1; challenges to 165–167; civil rights groups and 166–177; definition of 1, 9, 44, 169; economic transformations and 112–127; EEOC coverage and 72–87; empirical verification and 133; enforcement deregulation and 146, 148; equal employment opportunity and 1; expansion of the public sector workforce and 123; formal education and 72–87; goals and timetables and 170; Great Society and 15; group rights and 3; individual rights and 3; individualism and 2, 23; organizational arrangements and 128–144; personnel systems and 130, 141; state/local government and 91–111; cities/municipalities and 112–127; stigmatization of 2; stratification beliefs and 21–23
Aigner, D. 86, 88
Akron, OH 113
Almquist, E. 11
Anderson, B. 173
Anti-Recession Fiscal Assistance 114
Arrow, K. 89
Ashenfelter, O. 114, 125
Asian Americans: income of 104–108
Austin, TX 113, 120

Backoff, R.W. 129, 142
Barger, H. 115, 125
Barnett, M.R. 6
Beaumont, TX 118

Becker, G.S. 62, 70
Bell, D. 61, 70
Beller, A.H. 133, 142
Bellone, C.H. 142
Benokraitis, N.V. 10, 12, 19, 93, 108
Berkeley, CA 114, 118
Blacks/minorities: benign neglect 16; city employees and 115; economic transformations and municipal employment of 112–127; education/overeducation of 72–87; income of 72; labor markets and 68–69; labor shortages and 15; low-skill jobs and 116; organizational arrangements and employment of 128–140; public sector and 91–111; recent migrants to the sunbelt and 122; underclass 11; underrepresentation and 35; unemployment/employment and 61–91, 119
Blackstone, W.T. 10
Blau, F. 89
Blumberg, G. 130, 142
Borcher, R.R. 93, 108
Bradley, Justice 2
Brawner, J. 132, 143
Brown, M.K. 68, 70
Brown v. *Board of Education* 3
Buffalo, NY 113
Bureau of Labor 64
Burstein, P. 23, 72, 89, 133, 143

Cain, G. 86, 88
California 117
Campbell 141

181